cook school

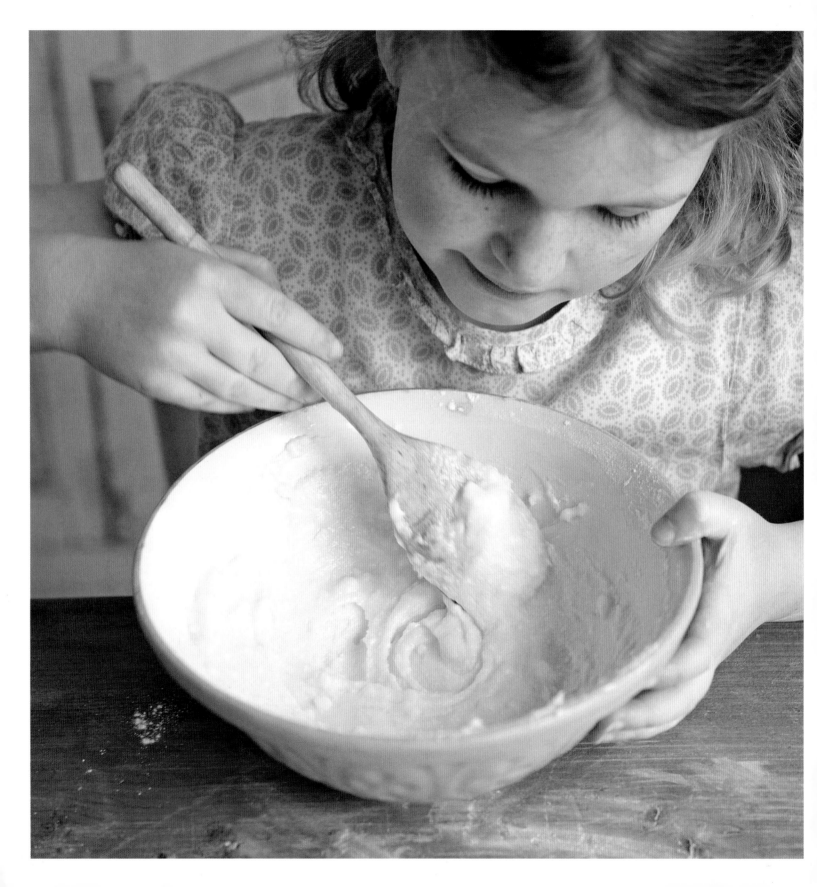

cook school

Amanda Grant

PHOTOGRAPHY BY SUSAN BELL

RYLAND
PETERS
& SMALL

LONDON NEW YORK

For Ethan and Noah, my two new, very special nephews and all the wonderful children who live in our street.

Senior Designer Iona Hoyle
Senior Editor Céline Hughes
Location Researcher Jess Walton
Production Toby Marshall
Publishing Director Alison Starling

Prop and Food Stylist Amanda Grant
Photoshoot Assistants Brenda Bishop and Esther Webb
Indexer Hilary Bird

First published in the UK in 2011
by Ryland Peters & Small
20–21 Jockey's Fields
London WC1R 4BW
www.rylandpeters.com

10 9 8 7 6 5 4 3 2 1

ISBN: 978-1-84975-135-3

A CIP record for this book is available from the British Library.

Printed in China

NOTES

• All spoon measurements are level unless otherwise specified.
• Ovens should be preheated to the specified temperatures. All ovens work slightly differently. We recommend using an oven thermometer and suggest you consult the maker's handbook for any special instructions, particularly if you are cooking in a fan-assisted oven, as you will need to adjust temperatures according to manufacturer's instructions.
• All eggs are medium, unless otherwise specified. It is recommended that free-range eggs be used.
• Recipes containing raw or partially cooked egg, or raw fish or shellfish, should not be served to the very young, very old, anyone with a compromised immune system or pregnant women.

Neither the author nor the publisher can be held responsible for any claim arising out of the information in this book. Always consult your health advisor or doctor if you have any concerns about your child's health or nutrition.

contents

Foreword by
Marguerite Patten, CBE

Cook School is a practical and inspiring cookery book for young children.

Amanda Grant has helped parents by producing excellent books on feeding children. Now she is showing children how to achieve a sense of achievement and pleasure by learning to cook.

The accepted method of teaching children to read is by giving them books, toys and information suitable for their age. This approach is followed in *Cook School*.

Interesting information and suitable recipes are given under the ages of 3–5 years, then 5–7 years and 7–11; in the case of food preparation, physical ability must also be considered.

Parents will be thrilled by the extra skills their children will develop.

Marguerite Patten

introduction

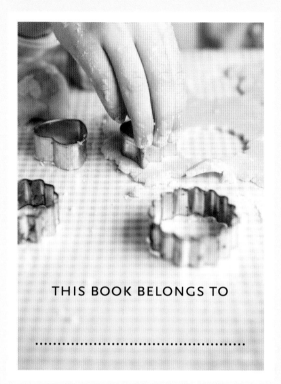

THIS BOOK BELONGS TO

....

Put your name in the space above and keep this book somewhere safe. Treasure it and enjoy it! You are about to learn some skills that you can use for the rest of your life. If you start cooking now, you will have lots of fun ahead of you making good food for you and your family and friends.

We all need to eat every day and it is much more exciting if you have helped to make some of those meals, instead of always eating food that others have made for you. Have you ever cooked a meal for anyone? When you do, you will see just how happy it makes people feel and how grateful they are for the time and care you have taken. This will make you feel proud too. It feels good when you cook for others.

THE SKILLS

Learning to cook is a bit like learning to read. When you learn to read, you learn the letters first and then you start to put the letters together to form words. It is similar to this when you learn to cook. You first learn some basic skills that you can later put together to make meals.

Cooking is not just about making something to eat; you will be practising maths (measuring, weighing, sharing); literacy (reading and writing if you jot down some notes about the recipes) and geography (learning about food and where it comes from) and much more.

Cooking uses all your senses. You can look at food, smell it, touch it, taste it and listen to it as it cooks. This is something my mum taught me when I was young. I think that's pretty exciting; I hope you do, too.

THE RECIPES

My children Ella, Lola and Finley have helped me to put this book together. They have guided me as to which recipes are the most fun to make and eat! They have also tested the recipes with the help of some friends, in particular Rosie, Libby and Tess.

The book has 3 main chapters – Stage 1 (3–5 years), Stage 2 (5–7 years) and Stage 3 (7–11 years). Even though the recipes in Stage 1 are suitable for children aged 3–5 years, if you are older than that and have just picked this book up you can still make the recipes from this section. The recipes in Stage 1 are great for mixing and matching with the other recipes in the book to make a complete meal. For example, crunchy paprika chicken (page 28) is great after pretty prawn cocktails (page 58) for a special supper, or three fruit salad (page 44) is a lovely pudding to have after pizzas (page 88).

I have included classic favourites like crumble topping (page 76), Victoria sponge (page 122), pastry (page 112), white sauce (page 96) and pizza dough (page 88). This is because I think that these are the basic building blocks for learning to cook. I was fortunate to be taught these recipes by my mother, my grandmother and my design technology teacher.

There are also lots of other exciting recipes in the book which use some ingredients that we are lucky enough to find in shops today. You can have a go at making your own sushi (page 102), you can see how to use corn tortillas (page 106), and you can have fun adding herbs and flowers to water to make your own ice bowl (page 70).

Remember that food is expensive, so don't be too disappointed if your parents don't want you to cook every day of the week. But the more you offer to make food that you can all eat as a family, the more likely it is that you will be able to cook, as your parents can include your food in their weekly budget.

THE PHOTOS

The children in the pictures in this book are friends of ours and they came to my kitchen to make the food you see in the photos. Some children asked if they could keep cooking in between having their photos taken, as they were enjoying it so much. For example, while Hector on page 112 was having his photo taken making toffee apple tarts, Sam was making the same tarts in the background because he didn't want to miss out!

YOUR NOTES

As you work your way through a recipe, try to think about it: did you like cooking it and would you like to cook it again? You might like to write some notes in the book. I know that normally you are told not to write in books, but this one is for you to keep forever and you might find it handy to jot down a few comments to remind you of something for next time. For example, would you add more herbs or spice to a recipe? Or make double the amount so that you have enough for friends to share, too?

WHY WE NEED TO EAT

The main reason why we need to eat good food is because it helps us to grow, develop and stay healthy. Ideally we need to eat 3 meals a day, with 2 small snacks in between. We also need to run around and play sport as much as possible, too, to help keep us fit and healthy.

There are certain types and amounts of food that we need to eat every day. We can eat everything, but we need to eat more of some foods than others. There are 5 main food groups:

1 Bread, rice, potatoes, pasta and other starchy foods
2 Fruit and vegetables
3 Milk and dairy foods
4 Meat, fish, eggs, beans and other non-dairy sources of protein
5 Foods and drinks that are high in fat and or sugar

Each day, ideally, we need to eat the following food:

Each meal or snack should contain a food from the bread, cereals and potatoes section. This means that we eat these foods 5 times a day.
1 portion = a bowl of breakfast cereal or 2 tablespoons of pasta or rice.

Each meal or snack should also contain a fruit or vegetable. We need 5 portions of fresh fruits and vegetables a day.

1 portion = 1 glass of fresh fruit juice, 1 piece of fruit, 2 tablespoons cooked vegetables.

3 portions of milk and dairy foods.
1 portion = 1 small glass of milk, 1 pot of yoghurt, 1 tablespoon grated cheese.

1 or 2 portions of meat, fish and alternatives a day.
1 portion = 2 pink fish fingers (page 60) or an oven-baked herby burger (page 64).

We don't need to eat foods from the fatty and sugary food section every day, as fats and sugars are often found in foods in the other food groups above, but we can have them as treats. Homemade cakes and biscuits are good for putting into packed lunches.

Did you know that all the food we eat comes from plants or animals? If possible, try to visit a local farm to see where animals are looked after and where crops are grown.

BEFORE YOU START COOKING

Always ask an adult before you start to make sure that they are happy you are cooking and to check that they will be around to help if you need it.

Try to find all the ingredients and the equipment that you will need for the recipe before you start. Oven gloves are especially important!

You might like to wear an apron. This can help keep the dirt from your clothes falling into the food and also stop the food that you cook going all over your clothes.

Wash your hands before you begin and dry them on a clean towel.

Always try to help clear up after you have made something, and help with the washing and drying up or loading the dishwasher. Your parents are far more likely to let you cook if you don't leave a huge mess behind.

This book is the beginning of your adventure with food and cooking!

Grown-ups: this page is for you

CHILDREN: YOU CAN SKIP THIS BIT AND HAVE FUN COOKING!

I am sure you already know this, but I can't stress enough how cooking with children at this stage can have a positive benefit on their development in so many areas. As much as possible, try to let your child complete each step of the recipe on her own to help her to gain a sense of independence in the kitchen.

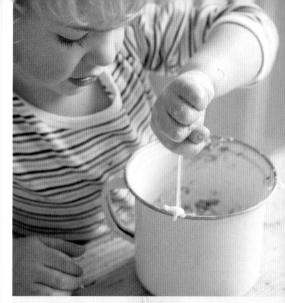

• Cooking will help your child with her physical development, for example her fine motor skills as well as her coordination of movement and eye-hand coordination. Just think about the range of physical skills that she needs to use scissors for cutting fresh herbs, to scoop flour from a container or bag or to brush melted butter onto pastry.

• She can measure with spoons and is likely to be able to learn to count. This is why all the ingredients in this section need to be counted or measured with spoons (except for the chocolate kisses).

• She will start to work out how to share food evenly, e.g. dividing the fruit between the pies (page 42).

• She will start to understand the concept of time, e.g. how long things take to set or cook.

• Encouraging your child to cook at this stage can be helpful, as she can make a snack (page 26) or dinner for the family (page 28). She will become more confident with the recipes the more she makes them.

• Her attention span will be increasing and she will be able to choose to stop an activity and then come back to it again later.

• She will begin to sort things into simple categories, become interested in what causes things to happen, and often ask 'why?'

• She will begin to be able to understand the concept of 'lots' or 'a little'; and she will be able to start to recognize primary colours.

• She will be able to help find the ingredients or equipment in the kitchen and match them to the pictures in the book.

• At this age, children love repetition. She will want to try the new skills over and over again.

• She is likely to be starting to enjoy the social element of sitting, talking and eating the food she has made with the rest of the family, and she can start to help with jobs like washing vegetables, laying the table and tidying away.

SKILLS

You might find these skills useful for other things that you do (not just cooking), like pouring water onto plants.

USING AN OVEN
Have you ever turned an oven on? Look at the recipe to see what temperature the oven needs to be at and then ask an adult to show you how to set the oven to that temperature. Most ovens have a little light that will go off when the oven has reached the right temperature. **Always use oven gloves when you are putting food in or taking food out of the oven.**

USING A SPOON TO SCOOP
For example, you could try scooping some flour from a big bowl into a little bowl.

STIRRING & MIXING
Try mixing ingredients together with different spoons, for example in the red dip on page 20.

COUNTING
Practise counting the number of spoonfuls or ingredients that you need.

SORTING
Look at the introduction on page 11 of the book to see the different categories of food. You could try sorting basic foods into each category.

SPREADING
Use a table knife to spread something soft like honey or butter onto toast. You will need to gently press the knife onto the food as you spread. Look at pages 26 and 27 for more spreading ideas.

POURING
Use small jugs that are not too heavy, for pouring liquids from one container to another.

CUTTING WITH A TABLE KNIFE
A table knife is the knife you use to eat your meal with. It is not sharp. Practise cutting something soft like butter or avocado with a table knife.

OPENING & CLOSING JARS
Try opening the lid on a jar. Some jars will be very stiff and you will need some help opening them.

DIPPING
Sometimes you will need to coat a food in a crisp coating to protect the food when it is being cooked and to give it a lovely, crisp texture.

CARRY WITHOUT SPILLING
Practise carrying liquids in containers without spilling them. The first time my son carried his lollies to the freezer with me when he was three years old we lost half the juice on the way to the freezer but now we hardly ever have any spillages!

WASHING FRUIT & VEGETABLES
Wash them in a bowl of water or put some water into the sink. It is a good idea to give salad vegetables and root vegetables, like carrots and potatoes that grow underneath the ground, a wash before they are eaten to remove the soil. Mickey had fun washing the vegetables for his dip on page 20.

DRAINING IN A COLANDER
A colander is like a bowl with holes in it. It is useful for draining food like vegetables after you have washed them.

MEASURING WITH SPOONS
The recipes will either say 'tablespoon', which is a big spoon or 'teaspoon', which is a small spoon. Make sure that you use the right spoon when you are measuring your ingredients.

SHARING
In some recipes you will need to make sure that you share the food evenly, like sharing the fillings between tarts. You don't want all of the filling in some of the tarts and none in the others!

FREEZING
Most homes have a freezer, even if it is very small. Freezers were invented to help keep food fresh for a long time without it going bad. How does food freeze? Most food contains lots of water. Freezing works by changing this water to ice. Put a liquid into a freezer and watch it change to a solid. The solid is called ice. See page 39 for ice lollies.

14

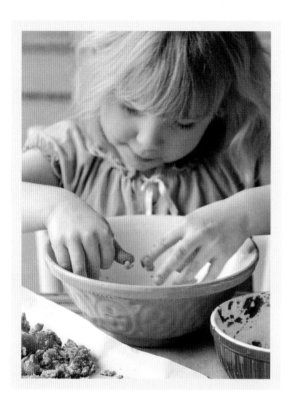

TOUCHING FOOD

When you touch food, think about how it feels – is it cold, slimy, hard or soft? On page 28 Lara loved touching the cold chicken and dipping it in the soft tomato purée and then the crunchy biscuits. Just remember never to lick your fingers after you have touched raw meat or fish.

MASHING

This is when you squash food using a potato masher, fork or pestle and mortar. Practise with soft fruits, e.g. page 36, or garlic, e.g. page 18.

TEARING

Try tearing some fresh herbs or salad leaves and then smelling them. My children like to smell mint, as they think it smells like toothpaste!

HULLING STRAWBERRIES

Use your fingers to pull the green stalks off the top of strawberries. You might need to dig your fingers into the fruit slightly so that you pull out the hard bit where the fruit and the stalk meet.

CUTTING WITH BISCUIT CUTTERS

Press the cutter into bread or pastry and twist it slightly to make sure that it cuts all the way through, and then lift the cutter up.

CUTTING WITH SCISSORS

Always make sure that your fingers stay away from the scissors so that you don't cut them accidentally.

BRUSHING

Use a pastry brush to brush milk, melted butter or oil. For example, brushing oil onto baking trays helps to stop the food from sticking to the trays.

ROLLING

Use a rolling pin to flatten something like bread (see page 22) or pastry (see page 42). When you roll pastry, try to roll small pieces of pastry, one at a time; it is much easier than rolling one big piece. Push the rolling pin down onto the pastry and roll it away from you.

SHAPING

Use your hands to mould the food into a shape. For example, for the strawberry sweets (page 38), you will need to mould the dough to make strawberry shapes. For the chocolate kisses (page 46), you need to mould the dough into small balls.

BASHING WITH A PESTLE

You don't have to have one of these, but if you do, try bashing a peeled clove of garlic to make the salad dressing on page 18.

CRUSHING GARLIC

Garlic grows in a 'bulb' with lots of small 'cloves' inside. Before you crush a clove of garlic you will need to peel it to remove the papery skin. Dig a fingernail into the skin to break it, then pull the skin away. To crush the clove put it in a garlic crusher and squeeze the crusher to close. You may need to scrape the crushed garlic off the crusher with a table knife. If you don't have a crusher, just bash the garlic with a rolling pin to release some of its juices and flavour and keep it whole.

LAYING THE TABLE

Have fun laying the table and clearing away. The fork sits on the left of the plate and the knife on the right. The knife blade faces towards the plate.

TASTING NEW FOODS

Try something new – you might like it. You will also need to taste the food that you have made to check that its tastes good before other people try it. Use a teaspoon to taste your food.

KITCHEN EQUIPMENT

These are a few things that you might find useful to have in the kitchen, however you don't need them all to do some cooking.

ROLLING PIN
These come in all different sizes, they are easy to use and great fun. They are needed for rolling out pastry or bread and they can be used for bashing olives to help remove their stones and bashing garlic cloves to help remove their skins!

CUTTERS
These come in all different shapes and sizes. Have fun cutting out circles of bread for the tasty bread tarts (page 34).

SIEVE
Why do we need to use a sieve? To remove any lumps and also to add air so that the food we cook or bake is light.

MIXING SPOONS
Wooden and melamine spoons are both great for mixing ingredients together.

PASTRY BRUSH
This is useful for brushing melted butter onto pastry, like the mini fruit pies on page 42 or for brushing oil onto baking trays e.g. the burgers on page 64 (if you are not using greaseproof paper).

PESTLE & MORTAR
You don't need one of these but they are fun to use for bashing food like cloves of garlic to make a dressing for a salad like on page 18. If you don't have one you can use a small rolling pin and a little bowl instead. The pestle is the stick and the mortar is the name given to the bowl.

POTATO MASHER OR FORK
This is for mashing soft fruit and vegetables.

MELON BALLER
If you don't have one of these, you can use a small teaspoon instead.

GARLIC CRUSHER
Peel the garlic clove first and then put the clove inside the garlic crusher. Push down to squeeze the garlic out (see page 15, above).

CHOPPING BOARD
Always wash your chopping board after you have used it. This is very important if you have used it to cut meat, poultry or fish.

MUFFIN TIN
You need this for the bread tarts on page 34 and you can also use it to make small cakes.

BAKING TRAY
These are very handy. For example, you will need one for the DIY pizzas on page 32, and many other things which you cook in the oven.

MIXING BOWL
These come in all different shapes and sizes. They are useful for so many different recipes, whether you are making a cake or mixing leaves together to make a salad.

COLANDER
This is like a sieve but it has bigger holes. It is great for draining things like cooked pasta or a jar of olives.

WIRE COOLING RACK
You don't have to have one of these, but it is useful for helping food to cool down.

SMALL JUG
Try to use small jugs for pouring, even if it means that you have to fill the jug up more than once.

FORK, TABLE KNIFE, SPOON
This is the cutlery that you use to eat with.

BIG & SMALL BOWL, PLATE
Hopefully this will not be too difficult to find in your kitchen cupboards.

OVEN
There are so many different types of ovens. Ask your parents to show you how yours works. Most ovens have a little light on them which will go off when the oven has reached the right temperature.

OVEN GLOVES
You can't cook safely without these. Whenever you help to put anything in or take anything out of the oven you must always put your oven gloves on! It is very easy to burn yourself.

SCISSORS
If you don't have kitchen scissors, use paper scissors to snip herbs but make sure that you wash them before and after you use them to cut up food. When you use scissors, always keep your fingers away from the blades so that you don't accidentally cut yourself.

MEASURING SPOONS
You will need 2 different sizes of spoon for recipes: a 'tablespoon', which is a big spoon, and a 'teaspoon', which is a small spoon. Make sure that you use the right spoon when you are measuring your ingredients.

salad bar with Susan's dressing

This is a recipe for a salad dressing. It is very useful to know how to make a good dressing so that you can always enjoy eating yummy salads. My friend Susan makes the best salad dressing and it tastes just like this. It is my children's idea to make a 'salad bar'. They like to choose salad ingredients from the fridge, put them into bowls and then we all help ourselves. Sometimes they choose things like grated carrot, tinned sweetcorn and crunchy bread croutons to go with the salad leaves.

SKILLS
◆ USING PESTLE & MORTAR
◆ MEASURING WITH SPOONS
◆ MIXING
◆ CUTTING WITH TABLE KNIFE
◆ WASHING
◆ POURING

1 To make Susan's dressing, peel the thin, pink skin away from the garlic clove and if you have a pestle and mortar, put the garlic into the bowl, add a tiny pinch of salt** and bash the garlic until you have a paste. If you don't have a pestle and mortar, crush the garlic in a garlic crusher and put into a jug, then use a small whisk to whisk everything together.

2 Add the mustard, balsamic vinegar and white wine vinegar and a little freshly ground black pepper and mix again.
3 Add the olive oil a little at a time – keep mixing all the time so that you end up with a smooth dressing. This will come with practice. Keep making it every time you have a salad!

For 4 people you need:

SUSAN'S DRESSING

1 garlic clove
tiny pinch of salt**
1 teaspoon mustard (English, wholegrain
or Dijon are all fine)
1 teaspoon balsamic vinegar
1 tablespoon white wine vinegar
a little freshly ground black pepper
6 tablespoons olive oil

SALAD INGREDIENTS

You can use any salad ingredients that
you like. Here are some that we often use:
ripe avocado* and cooked, peeled fresh
beetroot (you can chop these using a
table knife)
salad leaves e.g. lettuce leaves, rocket,
watercress, baby spinach leaves
cherry tomatoes, pitted olives, pine nuts,
small mozzarella balls

EQUIPMENT

pestle and mortar ◆ table knife
chopping board ◆ several small bowls
colander ◆ clean tea towel ◆ small jug

4 If you have some soft foods, like avocado* or beetroot, you
might like to cut these into small pieces using a table knife
and then put them into bowls.
5 Wash the lettuce in a colander in the sink, then shake or dry
with a clean tea towel. Put the lettuce in a bowl and then put
all your other salad ingredients into small bowls. Pour your
dressing into a jug. Let everyone help themselves to the pick
'n' mix salad bar. You will have some salad dressing left over to
use another day. Keep it in a clean jam jar in the fridge.

* Please ask an adult or older child to cut the avocado in half.
** I don't add salt to any recipes for children, but this is an
exception, as the salt helps you to mash the garlic to a paste.

STAGE
1

red dip
with crunchy veggies

Parents seem to like this dip just as much as the children do and it's a great way to try different vegetables, too. You could also make some corn chips from page 30 to eat with the dip. Mickey had great fun making this.

For 2–3 people you need:

INGREDIENTS
2 tablespoons tomato ketchup
4 tablespoons cream cheese
2 handfuls each: sugar snap peas, baby corn, small carrots and cherry tomatoes

EQUIPMENT
spoon ◆ mixing bowl ◆ bowl of water
clean tea towel ◆ small bowl ◆ plate

1 Count the spoons of tomato ketchup into a mixing bowl and then spoon the cream cheese into the bowl. You might need a small spoon to scrape the cream cheese from the big spoon. Mix to make an orangey-red mixture.
2 Wash the vegetables – put them in a bowl of water and wipe with your hands to get rid of any dirt or grit. If you clean the carrots really well, you won't need to peel them. Gently shake the vegetables to dry them or spread them on a clean tea towel to dry out.
3 Spoon the red dip into a small bowl and put it on a plate. Count the dry vegetables as you place them on the plate next to the dip. Now dip the vegetables into the dip and enjoy eating!

SKILLS
◆ WASHING
VEGETABLES
◆ USING SPOON
◆ COUNTING
◆ MIXING
◆ DIPPING

STAGE
1

roly-poly sandwich

Use a little smoked salmon as a treat in this sandwich, or you could use ham or salami instead. Try different types of bread like wholemeal, white or Granary. Have a look in your local bakery or supermarket at all the different kinds. If you have had fun making these sandwiches, you might like to try the Super Sushi Rolls on page 102, which are also rolled into pretty roly-poly shapes.

1 Put the slice of bread on a clean surface and use a table knife to cut the crusts off.
2 Flatten the slice of bread by rolling over it with a rolling pin.
3 Spread the cream cheese onto the bread with the table knife.
4 Lay the smoked salmon on top of the cream cheese and then sprinkle the mustard and cress over the salmon.
5 Starting with a short side of the bread slice, roll the bread up into a long sausage shape.

Cut the sausage shape with the table knife into 5 roly-poly sandwiches. When you lay them flat on a plate you'll see that you have made spirals!

Other filling ideas
A little tinned salmon or tuna, drained and mashed with a fork, mixed with a little mayonnaise, then scattered with a few torn lettuce or spinach leaves over the top. Or grated Cheddar cheese, ham torn into very small pieces and a finely chopped tomato.

For 1 roly-poly sandwich you need:

INGREDIENTS

1 slice brown, wholemeal, white or
Granary bread
1 tablespoon cream cheese
2 slices smoked salmon
a little mustard and cress

EQUIPMENT

table knife ◆ rolling pin ◆ small plate

SKILLS

◆ SPREADING
◆ ROLLING
◆ CUTTING WITH TABLE KNIFE

cheesy stuffed peppers

You need to choose small sweet peppers from your local greengrocer or a large supermarket for this recipe. These cheesy stuffed peppers are easy to make and eat and are great with some crusty bread for a packed lunch or a quick snack. Don't forget to smell the herbs as you spend some time choosing which ones to add to your cream cheese mixture. Maya made 5 stuffed peppers.

SKILLS MIXING ◆ SPOONING ◆ SMELLING HERBS

For 1 mini pepper you need:

INGREDIENTS
1 mini sweet pepper, top cut off (please ask an adult or older child to do this)
about 1 tablespoon cream cheese
2 teaspoons natural yoghurt
a few fresh herb leaves e.g. dill, thyme, sage or parsley

EQUIPMENT
mixing bowl ◆ spoon ◆ scissors

1 Use your fingers to scrape the little seeds out of the mini pepper.
2 Put the cream cheese and yoghurt in a mixing bowl and mix together with a spoon.

3 Pick the leaves off some herbs, or using scissors, snip the herb leaves into small pieces and add to the cream cheese mixture. Stir with the spoon. Spoon the cheese mixture into the pepper and put the lid back on top.

crunchy celery

This is a quick and easy snack that you can make all by yourself. It's also a good way to practise spreading, which will be useful when you make your own sandwiches and put jam, marmalade or honey on your toast for breakfast.

For 2 celery boats you need:

INGREDIENTS
1 celery stick, cut in half
a little peanut butter
10 dried cranberries, raisins or other dried fruit

EQUIPMENT
bowl of water • clean tea towel table knife

1 Wash the celery – put it in a bowl of water and wipe with your hands to get rid of any dirt or grit. Gently shake the celery to dry it or dry it with a clean tea towel.
2 Use a table knife to spread some peanut butter into the celery stick pieces.
3 Count 5 dried fruits and stick them onto the peanut butter.

SKILLS
♦ **WASHING VEGETABLES**
♦ **SPREADING**
♦ **COUNTING**

cucumber snacks

For an extra-quick snack you could try spreading some cream cheese onto cucumber slices and decorating them with pieces of dried apricot to make them look a bit like buttons. They taste yummy too!

For 4 buttons you need:

INGREDIENTS
4 slices cucumber
1 tablespoon cream cheese
1 dried apricot

EQUIPMENT
table knife ◆ scissors

1 Use a table knife to spread a little cream cheese on top of each cucumber slice.
2 Using scissors, snip the dried apricots into small pieces.
3 Dot the apricot pieces over the cream cheese, counting them as you go: how many pieces have you added?

SKILLS
◆ SPREADING
◆ COUNTING
◆ USING SCISSORS

STAGE
1

crunchy paprika chicken

Try this crispy chicken with different coatings, such as crunchy biscuits for cheese or breadcrumbs; my children like to dip the chicken into cornflakes (instead of biscuits) too.

For 4 people you need:

INGREDIENTS

about 10 dry biscuits for cheese – wheat are best (or 10 tablespoons cornflakes)
1 large pinch paprika
4 tablespoons tomato purée (or ketchup)
4 free-range skinless chicken thigh fillets, already cut into pieces (about 425 g)
salad and boiled new potatoes go well with the chicken

EQUIPMENT

scissors • greaseproof paper • 2 baking trays 2 mixing bowls • spoon • oven gloves

1 Turn the oven on to 180°C (350°F) Gas 4. Cut 2 pieces of greaseproof paper, each big enough to cover the baking trays, or brush a little olive oil over the trays. Count the biscuits into a mixing bowl and use your fingers to crush them into very small pieces. Add the paprika to the bowl, too, and mix with your hands.
2 Count the 4 spoonfuls of tomato purée and put them into another bowl.
3 Dip the chicken pieces into the tomato purée so that there is a bit of purée all over every piece.
4 Dip the pieces of chicken into the crushed biscuits so that the biscuit pieces stick to the chicken.
5 Put the crunchy chicken straight onto the lined baking trays. Now, WASH YOUR HANDS – you must always wash your hands thoroughly after handling raw meat.
6 Ask an adult to help you put the trays into the oven using oven gloves. Cook for 20 minutes or until the chicken is golden brown and cooked all the way through – ask an adult to help you check this.

SKILLS
◆ CRUSHING
◆ COUNTING
◆ DIPPING
◆ USING OVEN

green dip with corn chips

If you have friends round for tea you could have this as a starter instead of having a pudding. My son Finley and I created the corn chips when we found some slightly stale corn tortillas in our bread bin. He suggested that we cut them up and make them into crisps like we sometimes do with pita bread, so we did. They taste good!

SKILLS
- USING SCISSORS
- USING PESTLE & MORTAR
- USING TEASPOON
- MASHING

1 Turn the oven on to 180°C (350°F) Gas 4. Using scissors, snip the corn tortillas into small pieces and put on a baking tray. Ask an adult to help you put the tray into the oven using oven gloves. Bake for 5 minutes until golden and starting to crisp. Ask an adult to help you take the chips out of the oven.
2 Peel the garlic (see page 88 for help). If you have a pestle and mortar, put the garlic into the mortar (bowl) and bash with the pestle until you have a paste. If you don't have a pestle and mortar, use the end of a small rolling pin and a bowl.

Using scissors, snip the coriander into small pieces.
3 Add the coriander to the mortar (or bowl). Squeeze the juice from the lime half into the mortar. Mash with the pestle.
4 Scoop the stones out of the avocados with a teaspoon and peel away the skins.
5 Add some of the avocado flesh to the mortar and mash. Add the rest of the avocado flesh and mash again until you have a lumpy paste. Spoon the dip into a small bowl and serve with the corn chips.
* Please ask an adult or older child to cut the avocados in half.

For 4 people you need:
INGREDIENTS
4 corn tortillas
1 garlic clove
handful fresh coriander leaves
½ lime
2 ripe avocados, cut in half*
EQUIPMENT
*scissors • baking tray • oven gloves
pestle and mortar • spoon • small bowl*

DIY pizzas

This is one of my son Finley's favourite lunches which he has been making since he was three – the same age as Sholto in these pictures. I am a big fan of making pizzas using flour tortillas, muffins or French bread as they are quick and you can use any topping ingredients you have in the kitchen. My eldest daughter has even cooked these on a camp fire – you need to roll the tortilla up into a sausage first, wrap it in foil and ask an adult to put it on the fire for about 10 minutes.

To make 4 pizzas you need:

INGREDIENTS

4 flour tortillas, pieces French bread, muffins or bread rolls (all halved)

6 teaspoons tomato passata or tinned chopped tomatoes for each pizza

your choice of toppings (these are a few of our favourites):

grated cheese, tinned tuna, pitted olives, sweetcorn, pieces ham or salami, sliced pepper, sliced mushrooms, sliced cherry tomatoes

EQUIPMENT

scissors • greaseproof paper 2 baking trays • spoon oven gloves • chopping board • table knife

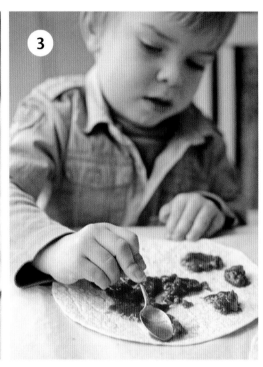

1 Turn the oven on to 200°C (400°F) Gas 6. Cut 2 pieces of greaseproof paper, each big enough to cover the baking trays. Put 2 tortillas on each baking tray.

2 Count 6 teaspoons of tomato passata onto each tortilla.

3 Use the back of the spoon to spread the passata over the tortillas but leave a little border around the edge so that it doesn't drip over the edges when the pizza is in the oven.

4 Choose some toppings and sprinkle them over the passata. Ask an adult to help you put the trays into the oven using oven gloves. Cook for 5 minutes. Ask an adult to help you take the cooked pizzas out of the oven using oven gloves and put them onto a chopping board. Using a table knife, cut them in half, then in half again to make quarters. Sholto liked to cut his pizza into quarters on his own and he said that it tasted very good.

SKILLS
◆ SPREADING
◆ CHOOSING
TOPPINGS
◆ CUTTING WITH
TABLE KNIFE
◆ USING OVEN

STAGE
1

tasty bread tarts

It can be frustrating if you want to cook something but you don't have the ingredients to do it. These tarts use basic ingredients that you should find in your kitchen like bread, milk and eggs. You can add other fillings like corn and tuna.

To make 6 tarts you need:

INGREDIENTS
a little unsalted butter
6 slices brown bread
3 free-range eggs and 4 tablespoons milk (or 2 eggs and 6 tablespoons milk)
handful fresh mint leaves (or other herbs) – have you ever smelt fresh mint leaves? They smell amazing!
2 handfuls frozen (and defrosted) or fresh peas or sweetcorn
small handful grated Parmesan

EQUIPMENT
scrap of greaseproof paper • muffin tin round cutter as wide as the slices of bread chopping board • oven gloves • table knife small jug • spoon • fork • scissors

1 Turn the oven on to 190°C (375°F) Gas 5. Take the round cutter and press it into each slice of bread on a chopping board to cut out 6 circles.
2 Using a scrap of greaseproof paper, rub some butter inside 6 of the holes in the muffin tin. Press each bread circle into the buttered muffin tin holes. Ask an adult to help you put the muffin tin into the oven using oven gloves. Bake for 5 minutes. Ask an adult to help you take the muffin tin out of the oven using oven gloves and leave to cool.
3 Now you need to crack open the eggs: hold an egg in one hand and carefully use a table knife to crack the egg in the middle. Put your thumbs into the crack and pull the egg shell apart. Let the egg fall into a jug. Repeat with the other eggs. (See page 60 for a photo of how to crack eggs.) Mix the eggs with a fork to break them up. Add the milk and mix the milk and eggs together with a fork again.

5

6

4 Using scissors, snip the mint into small pieces and put a little into each tart. Now put a few peas into each tart too – try to share them out evenly so that the tarts have roughly the same amount.

5 Slowly pour the egg mixture that's in the jug into the tarts over the peas and mint – try to stop pouring just before you reach the top, as the tarts will rise in the oven.

6 Sprinkle a little grated Parmesan over the tartlets. Ask an adult to help you put the muffin tin back in the oven using oven gloves. Cook for 12 minutes, or until they have puffed up and the egg is cooked.

SKILLS ◆ CUTTING SHAPES WITH CUTTERS AND SHARING TOPPINGS BETWEEN THE CASES.

◆ I HAVE ALSO SHOWN YOU HOW TO CRACK EGGS, WHICH IS IN THE NEXT SECTION OF THE BOOK, BUT YOU MIGHT LIKE TO START PRACTISING THIS SKILL NOW. DON'T WORRY IF SOME SHELL FALLS IN WITH THE EGG – JUST FISH IT OUT WITH A SPOON.

fizzy strawberry crush

This is great for practising mashing fruit and pouring using a jug. This drink is made with fizzy water, so you need to drink it straightaway before the bubbles disappear. If you don't like fizz, just add more fruit juice instead.

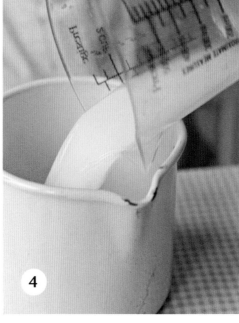

To make 2 glasses you need:

INGREDIENTS
2 large handfuls ripe strawberries
orange juice to half fill your glasses
fizzy water (or if you don't want fizz, add more juice or still water)

EQUIPMENT
bowl • potato masher • spoon • jug
2 glasses

1 Hull the strawberries – this means to pull the green stalks off the tops. You might need to dig your fingers into the strawberries to really pull the tops out.
2 Put the strawberries into a bowl and mash with a potato masher.
3 Spoon the strawberries into a jug.
4 Pour the orange juice onto the strawberries and mix with a spoon.
5 Pour the fizzy water into the jug, too and mix again with the spoon.
6 Pour the drink into 2 glasses. Drink straightaway and enjoy! If you haven't had a fizzy drink before, you might find that the bubbles feel funny in your mouth.

SKILLS
♦ HULLING STRAWBERRIES
♦ MASHING
♦ SPOONING
♦ POURING

5

6

Lola's strawberry sweets

Lola, my middle daughter, came up with this sweet idea. Even though these are quick to make, you will need to have some patience and wait for the sweets to dry after you have made them. This is just like playing with play dough!

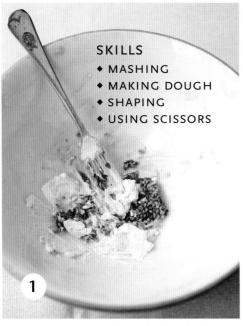

SKILLS
+ MASHING
+ MAKING DOUGH
+ SHAPING
+ USING SCISSORS

1

2

3

4

To make about 20 sweets you need:

INGREDIENTS
1 ripe strawberry (eat some more fresh strawberries while you're waiting for the sweets to set!)
1 tablespoon cream cheese
½ capful vanilla extract
about 300 g icing sugar (you may need slightly more or less to make a firm dough)
long thin green sweets to make strawberry 'stalks'

EQUIPMENT
mixing bowl + fork + greaseproof paper plate + scissors + pretty serving plate

1 Hull the strawberry – this means to pull the green stalk off the top using your fingers. Put the strawberry, cream cheese and vanilla into a mixing bowl and mash with a fork.

2 Add 3 spoonfuls of the icing sugar to the bowl and mix again. Add 3 more spoonfuls of sugar and keep mixing. You might want to use your hands now to mix. Keep adding sugar until you have a firm dough that is not too sticky.

3 Take a small piece of the mixture – about the size of a real strawberry – and shape it into a ball. Now squash it into a strawberry shape and put onto a plate. (You might like to put a piece of greaseproof paper on the plate first so that the sweets don't stick to the plate.) Take the fork and push it into the sweet to make holes. Repeat for the rest of the sweets.

4 Using scissors, cut the green sweets into short pieces, then cut a few slits into each piece so that they fan open to look like leaves. Push into the strawberry sweets and leave to dry for 3–4 hours. Transfer them to a pretty plate before you serve them!

stripey ice lollies

This is a great way to learn about freezing and watching liquid change to a solid. You can use old yoghurt pots or plastic cups, and wooden lolly sticks or plastic spoons. Don't use metal spoons as they will be too cold to hold when they freeze.

SKILLS
• POURING (JUICE INTO MOULDS)
• FREEZING (CHANGING TEXTURE)

To make as many as you like you need:

INGREDIENTS
purple fruit juice (I used blackcurrant but you could also try a red fruit juice like raspberry)

cloudy apple juice

EQUIPMENT
old yoghurt pots and the same number of wooden lolly sticks or plastic spoons (or lolly moulds) • you will also need to make sure there is room in your freezer to stand all your yoghurt pots or lolly moulds

1 Find some old yoghurt pots and make sure that they are clean and dry. You will also need some wooden lolly sticks or plastic spoons – you should have enough of these to go in all your yoghurt pots. Put one lolly stick or spoon into each yoghurt pot. Start pouring the purple fruit juice into a yoghurt pot until it's half full. Repeat this with all your other yoghurt pots. You might like to pour the purple juice first into some of the pots and the apple juice first into the other pots so that the stripes look different when the lollies are frozen.

2 Put the pots into the freezer and freeze until frozen – this will take at least 4 hours. Take the pots out of the freezer and pour the other juice over the frozen juice until you nearly reach the top of the pot. Don't fill them too full!

3 Put the pots back into the freezer and freeze again for 4 hours or until you have frozen ice lollies. When you take the lollies out of the freezer, you might need to sit each one in a little warm water to help ease the lolly itself out of the pot, but don't leave it sitting in the warm water for long otherwise it will melt.

STAGE
1

berry crunch

This is like a fruit fool (which is a creamy yoghurt) but with some crunch added. It makes a wonderful breakfast, pudding or snack. The amounts in this recipe are only a guide, as the exact quantities will vary depending on the size of glasses that you decide to use.

For 2 glasses you need:

INGREDIENTS
4 handfuls fresh berries
4 tablespoons natural Greek yoghurt
8 tablespoons crunchy cereal or muesli

EQUIPMENT
bowl • fork • spoon • 2 glasses

1 Put most of the berries into a bowl (save a few for decorating the top) and mash with a fork or potato masher.
2 Count the spoons of yoghurt into the bowl with the mashed berries and mix with the spoon.
3 Spoon a bit of the cereal into the bottom of the glasses and spoon the fruity yoghurt on top of the cereal. You will start to see layers in the glasses.

Spoon a little more cereal on top of the yoghurt and then dollop some more yoghurt on top of the cereal. Finish with the saved berries on top.

SKILLS
◆ MASHING
◆ SPOONING
◆ MIXING

mini fruit pies

Ready-made puff pastry is just right for these mini fruit pies. When you are rolling pastry, it is much easier to roll one small piece at a time instead of rolling one large piece, which is why I have broken the pastry into 4 pieces. These pastries taste delicious and are good for packed lunches, a teatime treat or pudding. If you choose to use big dried fruits like mango or apricots, you will need to use scissors to cut them into small pieces first.

1

2

3

1 Turn the oven on to 180°C (350°F) Gas 4. Cut a piece of greaseproof paper big enough to cover the baking tray. Put the melted butter, dried fruits and spice in a mixing bowl and mix with a spoon.
2 Break the pastry in half, then break each piece in half to make 4 pieces. Sprinkle a little flour on the work surface. Flatten one piece of pastry with a rolling pin until it is about the same thickness as a pound coin.
3 Take the round cutter and, starting at the edge of the pastry, push it down to cut out circles. Keep going until you have used up all of that pastry. Roll out another piece of pastry and cut out circles. Repeat

with the rest of the pastry. Using a teaspoon, spoon a little fruit mixture onto the middle of each circle. Bring the edges of the circle up together to seal the mixture inside. There should be no gaps in the pastry!
4 Turn the parcels over and flatten slightly with your hand. Using a table knife, carefully cut 2 or 3 short slits in the top of each pastry – this will let the steam escape when the pastries are baking.
5 Put them on the baking tray. Dip a pastry brush in a little melted butter and brush over all the pies. Sprinkle with sugar. Ask an adult to help you put the tray in the oven and bake for 15 minutes. They should look golden!

To make 16 mini pies you need:

INGREDIENTS
small piece of butter, about the size of 2 pieces of chocolate, melted (ask an adult or older child to do this), plus a little extra
20 tablespoons (200 g) dried fruits
1 teaspoon mixed spice
375 g puff pastry
a little flour for sprinkling
a little demerara sugar or golden caster sugar

EQUIPMENT
scissors • greaseproof paper • baking tray • mixing bowl • spoon • rolling pin • pound coin • round cutter about 6 cm across • spoon • table knife • pastry brush

SKILLS
♦ MIXING
♦ ROLLING PASTRY
♦ CUTTING CIRCLES
♦ BRUSHING
♦ USING OVEN

STAGE
1

three fruit salad

Have you ever made melon balls before? It's great fun scooping the melon flesh into balls. A melon baller doesn't cost very much to buy – just look in any good cook shop. If you don't have a melon baller, you can use a small teaspoon. You can make a fruit salad with other fruits as well, like strawberries, raspberries and sliced peaches. It's tasty, colourful and good for you, too!

For 3 people you need:

INGREDIENTS
½ ripe melon (seeds removed)
2 satsumas
1 ripe banana
150 ml orange and mango juice
(or other juice of your choice)

EQUIPMENT
melon baller or small rounded teaspoon
pretty bowl ◆ table knife ◆ spoon

1

2

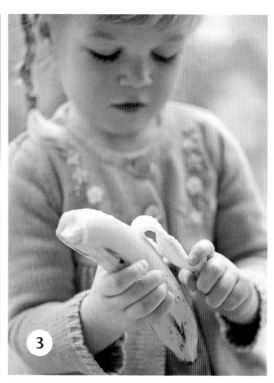
3

1 Use a melon baller or a teaspoon to scoop out small balls of melon flesh and put into a pretty bowl for the fruit salad.
2 Peel the satsumas and then, using a table knife, cut each segment in half. Add to the bowl of melon balls.
3 Peel the banana and put the skin on the compost heap, if you have one.

4 Using the table knife again, cut the banana into small pieces. Add to the bowl.
5 Pour the juice over the fruit and stir together.

SKILLS
◆ USING MELON BALLER
◆ POURING

4

5

chocolate kisses

This is the first recipe in the book that needs the ingredients to be weighed. There is more information about weighing in Stage 2 of the book. If you weigh everything before you start cooking, the rest is very easy.

To make 25 kisses you need:

INGREDIENTS
200 g unsalted butter – soft
100 g golden caster sugar
capful vanilla extract
250 g self-raising flour
2 tablespoons cocoa powder

RASPBERRY CREAM
4 ripe raspberries
100 g unsalted butter – soft
100 g icing sugar

EQUIPMENT
scrap of paper • 2 baking trays • mixing bowl
wooden spoon • oven gloves • small bowl • fork

1 Turn the oven on to 180°C (350°F) Gas 4. Take a scrap of paper and use it to rub a little butter over 2 baking trays.
2 Put the soft butter, sugar and vanilla extract in a mixing bowl and mix well with a wooden spoon until it becomes fluffy and paler in colour. This helps to beat air into the mixture.
3 Tip the flour and cocoa powder into the bowl and mix well with your hands.
4 Break the mixture into 5. Now break each piece into 10 pieces, all the same size. Roll each piece into small balls about the size of a small walnut, then flatten a bit. Put onto the baking trays and ask an adult to help you put them in the oven using oven gloves. Bake for 6–7 minutes, then ask an adult to help you take the trays out of the oven. Leave to cool.
5 For the raspberry cream, put the berries into a small bowl, mash with a fork, then add the butter and icing sugar and mix with the fork.
6 Spoon a little cream onto a kiss and sandwich with another kiss. Keep going until you have 25 kisses.

SKILLS

◆ BUTTERING BAKING TRAYS
◆ INTRODUCTION TO CREAMING
BUTTER AND SUGAR (SEE PAGE 51)
◆ SHAPING
◆ MASHING

5

6

STAGE
1

Grown-ups: this page is for you

CHILDREN: YOU CAN SKIP THIS BIT AND HAVE FUN COOKING!

As your child works through these recipes, help him to link them up with recipes and skills from the previous chapter. He could make the red dip as a starter (page 20), then the oven-baked herby burgers from this chapter for the main course.

◆ At some point during this stage, he is likely to be ready to learn how to use a small, sharp knife for cutting, but make sure that you always stay with him and guide him to follow safe cutting techniques.

◆ Your child will be more aware of size, shape and weight. Encourage him to guess the weights of random objects and then weigh them to see what the result is. Also encourage him to weigh all the ingredients for a recipe before he starts cooking.

◆ He will be growing towards reading and writing independently. Encourage him to read some of the words and to follow the sequence of steps for the recipes with the photos to guide him.

◆ He will be more willing to work out what he needs to do next, so try to avoid the temptation to tell him. As much as possible, let him work through recipes on his own.

◆ He will be more expressive with his language and more willing to share what he thinks of a recipe. After he has made something, ask him about it, e.g. if he would change anything if he made it again.

◆ He will start to show an interest in the science behind food and will enjoy watching food like couscous change from small, inedible hard pellets to something soft that is good to eat.

◆ He will be ready to use more complex kitchen equipment, like graters or lemon juicers.

◆ Encourage him to use his imagination by adding his own ingredients e.g. other toppings to the tomato tarts on page 56.

◆ He will be able to help work out how long the food needs to cook in the oven and how to share the food evenly between the whole family.

◆ He will have an increased interest in the world around him and where food comes from. Help him to understand that all the food we eat comes from plants and animals and that some of these plants grow in other countries.

◆ He will want to help with simple tasks like laying the table and clearing away, and this will help with his social development.

SKILLS

I hope that you enjoyed learning the skills in Stage 1. Here are some more to have fun practising as you cook some new recipes.

USING A GRILL

Does your oven have a grill? Most ovens do. When you turn it on, the element will heat up until it is red. If you put some food underneath the grill, like the bagel on page 66, the grill will toast it until it is golden and bubbling. **Always use oven gloves when you are putting food under or removing food from the grill.**

KNIVES

Always ask an adult before you use a sharp knife. It is likely that you will be ready now, with help from an adult, to use a small paring knife. The safest and most popular ways to use a knife are the bridge-cutting and claw-cutting techniques.

BRIDGE-CUTTING TECHNIQUE

Hold the food between a thumb and finger of one hand to make a bridge. Hold a small paring knife in the other hand, put the blade under the bridge and cut downwards through the food.

CLAW-CUTTING TECHNIQUE

Make your fingers into a 'claw' shape, tucking your thumb inside your fingers. Use this claw to hold the food. Hold a small paring knife in your other hand and cut the food. As the knife moves along the food, pull the claw away from the knife.

GRATING

Hold the handle of the grater with one hand and then push the cheese downwards over the grater 'teeth'. Always keep your fingers away from the grater 'teeth', as they are very sharp.

LINING A BAKING TIN

You will need to sit the tin on the paper first and draw around it before you cut it with scissors. If you do this, the paper should fit inside the tin.

MEASURING

Have you ever measured a liquid before? Fill a jug with water. You will then need a measuring jug: this is a jug with measurements written up the side. Carefully pour water into the measuring jug, up to the level that you need e.g. 150 ml.

MEASURING VOLUME

If you want to work out the 'volume' of a container (that is how much liquid the container will hold), first fill it with water, then pour this water into a measuring jug. Write down the level on the measuring jug on a piece of paper. You then know how much liquid you need to fill the container. You could practise this by making some stripey ice lollies – see recipe on page 39.

WEIGHING

Learn how to use weighing scales. All scales are different, so you will need to ask an adult to show you how to use yours. Why don't you have a go at weighing some fruits or vegetables e.g. a banana or 2 apples. You could also see if you can guess how much you think something will weigh and then put it on the scales to see what the result is.

SHARING & DIVIDING

When you have made a large quantity of mixture, you may need to divide it up into small amounts before you cook it. For example, for the burgers on page 64, you need to divide the mixture into 8 equal pieces. To do this, first cut the mixture into 2 equal pieces (halves), then cut each half in half to make 4 equal pieces (quarters) and then cut each quarter in half again to make eighths.

SHAPING

Use your hands to help you shape any mixture.

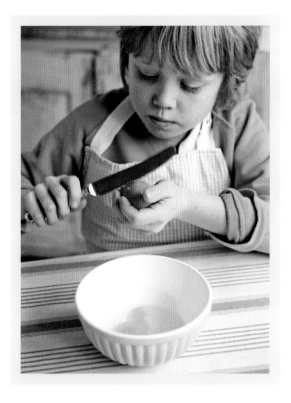

HOW TO CRACK AN EGG

There are 2 ways to crack eggs. Either hold an egg in one hand and carefully use a table knife to crack the egg in the middle. Put your thumbs into the crack and pull the egg shell apart. Let the egg fall into a jug or bowl and mix with a fork. Fish out any egg shell with a spoon. Or, if you prefer, you can crack an egg by bashing it on the side of a bowl, but you might end up with some of the egg dripping down the side of the bowl until you've had a chance to practise! Always wash your hands well after cracking eggs, as it is very easy to pass bacteria from raw food like eggs to cooked food.

OPENING TINS

This will take some practice and you need to be careful, as tins are sharp. Ask an adult to show you how to use your tin opener, as they all differ.

MELTING CHOCOLATE & BUTTER

Heat the chocolate and butter very, very gently in a saucepan over low heat so that the chocolate melts slowly.

RUBBING BUTTER INTO FLOUR

Once you know how to rub fat into flour you can make pastry, crumble toppings or biscuits. Make sure that the butter is really cold. Use a table knife to cut the cold butter into small pieces, add to the flour and gently rub the pieces of butter between the tips of your thumbs and fingers so they flatten and gradually mix into the flour. Keep lifting your fingertips above the bowl, as this will let air get to the flour and keep the mixture cool. Try not to use your whole hands, as this will melt the butter.

CREAMING BUTTER & SUGAR

The most common way to make cakes and many biscuits is to begin by creaming together softened butter with sugar – this means beating the sugar and butter together either with a wooden spoon or an electric mixer until the mixture is very pale and fluffy. This adds air to the mixture and gives it a light and fluffy, almost mousse-like texture. Before you begin: use unsalted butter (it has a better flavour than margarine) and you will need to take it out of the fridge some time before you start so that it is soft. If the butter is too hard you will not be able to beat in a lot of air and the cake may not rise as well.

FOLDING

This is when you carefully mix a cake mixture, almost cutting it with the spoon to 'fold' it rather than mix it. This method adds air to the mixture so that it stays light and airy. It is easier if you use a metal spoon instead of a wooden spoon.

BREADCRUMBING

Dip the food into a little beaten egg, then dip into breadcrumbs and turn to coat the food evenly.

MARINATING

A marinade can actually start to soften food and break it down, so do you need to be careful how long you leave the food sitting in marinade. For example, fish left to marinate in lemon juice and oil will start to cook as it sits in the lemon juice.

KITCHEN EQUIPMENT

There's lots more to explore in the kitchen now that you are getting used to cooking and using different types of equipment. Here are a few that might be good to try.

WEIGHING SCALES

The great thing with cooking is that you can practise things you are learning at school, like maths, when you measure and weigh out ingredients. Ask your parents if they have a set of weighing scales that you can use. There are lots of different types, so ask an adult to show you how to use them.

GARLIC CRUSHER

This is easy and good fun to use. Make sure that you peel the pink skin away from the garlic clove before you crush it.

GRATER

Remember that the small 'teeth' can be as sharp as little knives, so make sure that you always keep your fingers away from them. Graters come in different shapes and sizes and the 'teeth' on the graters vary in size.

PALETTE KNIFE

This is handy for lifting things.

MEASURING JUG

Most measuring jugs have markings up to 500 ml.

SAUCEPANS

Ideally you need a small saucepan for pasta sauces and a large pan for cooking pasta (see page 94).

SMALL, SHARP KNIFE

A small paring knife is the best knife to begin with. Once you know how to hold your knife and cut food safely, there are so many things that you can make to eat. The two main cutting techniques are the 'bridge' and the 'claw' techniques (see page 50, above). Once you have learnt how to master these, you can cut most things safely, but always ask an adult before you use a sharp knife.

SPATULA

This is ideal for scraping a bowl clean, but you might prefer to use your fingers (if the mixture is safe to eat – check with an adult)!

TIN OPENER

Some foods come in tins and some tins have a ring pull, which makes them easy to open. Others will require a tin opener. Let an adult help you the first time you use one.

LEMON JUICER

If you don't have a juicer, cut the fruit into smaller pieces and squeeze the juice out by hand. You will probably need to sieve the juice to make sure that you remove any pips.

KETTLE

Make sure an adult or older child helps you with this. You only need the kettle for one recipe in this chapter – the couscous recipe on page 62.

BAKING TINS

Loaf tins, small round tins or square tins are all used to bake cakes.

ROUND CUTTER

This is helpful for cutting out biscuits or small tarts like on page 56 but if you don't have a cutter, use a small cup or bowl instead.

OVENPROOF DISH

You will need a dish that won't crack when you put it into the oven for recipes like the what's-in-season fruit crumble on page 76.

herby scrambled eggs

Did you know that the yolk of the egg is orange and the clear part is called the white? Scrambled eggs are a great, simple recipe to learn, as once you know how to make them, you can make them for your lunch, breakfast or supper.

For 1 person you need:

INGREDIENTS
fresh herb e.g. parsley leaves or chives
2 free-range eggs
4 cherry tomatoes
a little unsalted butter
buttered toast, to eat with the eggs

EQUIPMENT
scissors ◆ mixing bowl ◆ table knife
spoon ◆ fork ◆ small paring knife
saucepan ◆ pan stand

1 Using scissors, snip some herbs into small pieces and put in a mixing bowl. Now you need to crack open the eggs: hold an egg in one hand and carefully use a table knife to crack the egg in the middle. Put your thumbs into the crack and pull the egg shell apart. Let the egg fall into the bowl. Repeat with the other egg. Fish out any egg shell with a spoon. (See page 60 for a photo of how to crack eggs.) Mix with a fork.

2 Use the bridge-cutting technique to cut the tomatoes: make a 'bridge' with a thumb and finger of one hand and hold the tomato. Hold a small paring knife in your other hand and put the blade under the bridge, then cut downwards firmly. Now cut each half into quarters and add to the eggs.

3 Put the butter in a saucepan. Melt over medium (not high) heat. Add the eggs and cook, stirring with a spoon. Keep stirring to break up the egg.

4 When the eggs are almost cooked – so they look only slightly wet – take the pan off the heat and rest it on a pan stand. Keep stirring until the eggs are cooked – the heat from the pan will continue to cook them. Eat with toast.

STAGE
2

mini puffy tomato tarts

SKILLS
- ROLLING PASTRY
- CUTTING CIRCLES
- SPREADING
- CHOOSING TOPPINGS
- USING OVEN

Thanks to Libby and Tess for testing this recipe. They found it great fun rolling out the pastry, cutting out circles and spreading the pesto on top. If you haven't used a grater before, make sure that you keep your fingers away from the sharp 'teeth'.

To make 10 mini tarts you need:

INGREDIENTS

3 big handfuls ripe cherry tomatoes
35 g Cheddar cheese
200 g puff pastry
a little flour for sprinkling
4–5 teaspoons pesto (or sun-dried tomato paste)
you could also try other toppings like chopped olives, chorizo or salami

EQUIPMENT

chopping board ◆ small paring knife grater ◆ rolling pin ◆ pound coin ◆ round cutter about 7 cm across ◆ 2 non-stick baking trays ◆ spoon ◆ oven gloves

1 Use the bridge-cutting technique to cut the tomatoes: on a chopping board, make a 'bridge' with a thumb and finger of one hand and hold the tomato. Hold a small paring knife in your other hand and put the blade under the bridge, then cut downwards firmly. Now cut each half into quarters.
2 To grate the cheese, hold the handle of the grater with one hand and use the other hand to push the cheese downwards over the grater 'teeth'. Always keep your fingers away from the grater 'teeth' as they are very sharp.
3 Break the pastry in half. Sprinkle a little flour on the work surface. Roll one piece of pastry with a rolling pin until it is about the same thickness as a pound coin.
4 Take the round cutter and, starting at the edge of the pastry, push it down into the pastry to cut out circles. Keep going until you have used up all of that pastry. Roll out the other piece of pastry and make more circles.

5 Put the pastry circles on the baking trays. Use a teaspoon to spread a bit of pesto over each pastry circle. Try to leave a little border around the edge of the circles – this will help the pastry to puff up around the pesto when it cooks.
6 Put a few pieces of tomato on top of the pesto and, if you like olives, chorizo or salami, chop some and add those too. Sprinkle the grated cheese over the tarts. Ask an adult to help you put the trays into the oven using oven gloves. Cook for 15 minutes. The pastry should be cooked and slightly puffy and the cheese will have melted.

STAGE
2

pretty prawn cocktails

This is a great lunch, or if you want to have a special meal you could make this for a starter instead of having a pudding. Did you know that prawns are grey when they are raw and they turn pink when they are cooked?

For 4 people you need:

INGREDIENTS
4 tablespoons mayonnaise
2 tablespoons tomato ketchup
¼ lemon
about 10 crisp lettuce leaves
250 g cooked, peeled prawns
a little paprika

EQUIPMENT
spoon ◆ small bowl ◆ colander ◆ clean tea towel ◆ 4 small plates or bowls

1 Count the spoons of mayonnaise and ketchup into a small bowl.
2 Squeeze the juice from the lemon quarter into the bowl and mix everything together with the spoon to make a pink sauce.
3 Put the lettuce in a colander and wash in the sink. Gently shake the lettuce to dry it or spread it on a clean tea towel to dry out. Tear the lettuce into big chunks.
4 Share the chunks of lettuce between 4 small plates or bowls, then share the prawns out evenly too, and put them on top of the lettuce. Spoon a little pink sauce on top of each. Take a small pinch of paprika with your fingers and sprinkle over each prawn cocktail.

SKILLS
◆ COUNTING
◆ SQUEEZING LEMONS
◆ WASHING VEGETABLES
◆ DIVIDING

pink fish sandwich

You can make these whenever you have some spare time in the day and then keep them in the fridge until you are ready to cook them. Instead of adding lemon zest to the breadcrumb mixture you could try lime, or to make green fish fingers add lots of fresh chopped herbs to the breadcrumbs. All three of my children insisted that this recipe went in the book, as they love making them with their friends!

For 4 people you need:

INGREDIENTS

8 thin salmon fillets (or white fish like haddock), cut into strips by an adult
2 free-range eggs
about 8 tablespoons breadcrumbs
1 unwaxed lemon or lime or handful fresh herbs
8 tablespoons plain flour
8 thick slices bread, some sliced tomatoes and watercress or lettuce

EQUIPMENT

scissors • greaseproof paper
2 baking trays • table knife
3 small bowls • spoon • fork
small grater • oven gloves

1 Turn the oven on to 190°C (375°F) Gas 5. Cut 2 pieces of greaseproof paper, each big enough to cover the baking trays. Rub your finger all over the fish to check for bones. If you feel a sharp bone sticking out, pull it out with your fingers.
2 To crack open the eggs, hold an egg in one hand and carefully use a table knife to crack the egg in the middle. Put your thumbs into the crack and pull the egg shell apart. Let the egg fall into a small bowl. Repeat with the other egg. Fish out any egg shell with a spoon. Mix with a fork.

3 Put the breadcrumbs into a small bowl. To grate the lemon or lime, hold the handle of the grater with one hand and use the other hand to push the fruit downwards over the grater 'teeth'. Always keep your fingers away from the grater 'teeth', as they are very sharp. Add the zest to the breadcrumbs.
4 Count the spoons of flour into a small bowl. Dip the fish first into the flour, then the beaten egg, then the breadcrumbs so that the fish is well coated. Put the fish pieces on the baking trays.

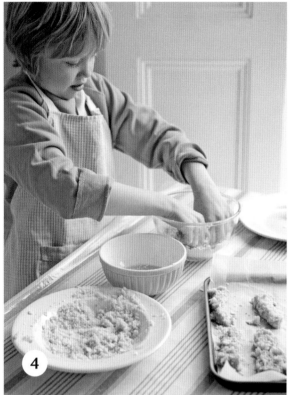

4

Ask an adult to help you put the trays into the oven using oven gloves. Cook for 10–15 minutes or until the fish is golden and cooked all the way through – ask an adult to help you check this. Ask an adult to help you take the trays out of the oven using oven gloves. Put the fish pieces inside some bread with sliced tomatoes and watercress.

SKILLS
- BREADCRUMBING
- CRACKING EGGS
- USING OVEN
- ZESTING LEMON

STAGE
2

minty lamb couscous

This is great to make after you have had roast lamb at the weekend. However, if you haven't had a roast, you could try adding other ingredients instead like tinned fish, crumbled feta cheese, chopped tomatoes, fresh herbs, chopped cucumber, watercress, grated carrot etc. and then mix with Susan's salad dressing from page 18 instead of the mint jelly.

For 4 people you need:

INGREDIENTS
200 g couscous
225 ml boiling water (or just enough to cover the couscous)
2 large handfuls dried apricots
1 large courgette or 2 small courgettes
about 3 teaspoons mint jelly
a few handfuls leftover roast lamb, chopped
freshly ground black pepper, if you like

EQUIPMENT
heatproof bowl • measuring jug • fork • scissors • grater

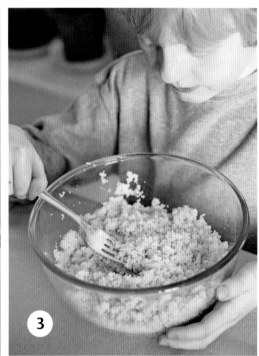

1 Weigh the couscous. How you weigh it will depend on the weighing scales that you use. (See pages 50 and 52 for more information about how to weigh ingredients.) Put the couscous into a heatproof bowl.

2 Ask an adult or older child to boil the kettle and pour the boiling water into a measuring jug up to the 250-ml mark. Pour this water carefully over the couscous. Leave the couscous for about 5 minutes and watch as the hard grains absorb the hot water and become soft and fluffy.

3 Use a fork or your hands to mix the couscous and break up the grains. The grains will feel lovely and soft!

4 Using scissors, snip the apricots into small pieces. To grate the courgettes, hold the handle of the grater with one hand and use the other hand to push the courgette downwards over the grater 'teeth'. Always keep your fingers away from the grater 'teeth', as they are very sharp. Add the courgettes and apricots to the couscous. Add the mint jelly and chopped roast lamb to the couscous and mix everything together. Taste the mixture and add a little black pepper if you think it needs it.

SKILLS • PREPARING COUSCOUS • MEASURING LIQUID
USING SCISSORS • GRATING

4

oven-baked herby burgers

Lots of children have helped to test the recipes in this book, especially Rosie, Libby and Tess. They all felt that the book should have a burger recipe in it and they found this oven-baked burger recipe easy to cook and good to eat.

1 Turn the oven on to 190°C (375°F) Gas 5. Dip a pastry brush into a little olive or vegetable oil and brush it all over a baking tray. This will stop the burgers from sticking to the tray.

2 Using a table knife, cut the cheese into small pieces on a chopping board.

3 Using scissors, snip the herb into small pieces and put into a mixing bowl. Still using scissors, snip the ends off the spring onions and throw away, then snip the onions into tiny pieces and put in the bowl.

4 Now you need to crack open the egg: hold it in one hand and carefully use a table knife to crack the egg in the middle. Put your thumbs into the crack and pull the egg shell apart. Let the egg fall into a small bowl. Fish out any egg shell with a spoon. (See page 60 for a photo of how to crack eggs.) Mix with a fork.

5 Put the beef mince, chopped cheese and egg into the bowl with the herbs and onions and mix everything together really well with your hands.

6 Break the beef mixture in half and then break each piece in half again to make 4 pieces (quarters). Now break each quarter in half again to make 8 pieces (eighths). Roll each piece into a ball with your hands, then put onto the oiled baking tray and flatten into a burger shape. Do the same with all the

To make 8 small burgers you need:

INGREDIENTS
a little olive or vegetable oil
about 35 g Cheddar cheese
small handful fresh herbs e.g. parsley,
coriander or thyme
2 spring onions
1 free-range egg
500 g good-quality beef mince
(don't buy extra-lean mince otherwise
your burger will be too dry)
8 bread rolls, some lettuce, sliced
tomatoes and tomato ketchup

EQUIPMENT
pastry brush • baking tray • table knife
chopping board • scissors • mixing bowl
small bowl • spoon • fork • palette knife
oven gloves

pieces. Now, WASH YOUR HANDS – you
must always wash your hands thoroughly
after handling raw meat. Ask an adult to
help you put the tray into the oven using
oven gloves. Cook for 8 minutes. Ask an
adult to help you take the tray out of the
oven using oven gloves. Using a palette
knife, turn the burgers over and put back in
the oven for 8 more minutes or until cooked
in the middle. Eat in bread rolls with lettuce,
tomatoes and ketchup.

Tip: To make lamb burgers, swap the beef
for lamb and add thyme leaves, plus snipped
dried apricots instead of Cheddar cheese.

SKILLS
• CHOPPING WITH TABLE KNIFE
• USING SCISSORS
• CRACKING EGGS
• COUNTING
• DIVIDING
• SHAPING
• USING OVEN

STAGE
2

grilled ham bagel

Help your parents out by making your own snack or lunch. Just remember that the grill is hot and you must have an adult with you when you use it. Choose a favourite relish or chutney to spread over the top. If your bagel is for lunch, try to have some chopped cucumber, celery or carrot with it. It is a good idea to have a vegetable or fruit with every meal and snack, so that you eat your '5 a day'.

To make 1 bagel you need:

INGREDIENTS
1 bagel, cut in half
1 slice ham
small piece Cheddar cheese
chutney, if you like

EQUIPMENT
*baking tray • grater • oven gloves
table knife*

SKILLS
- ◆ USING GRILL
- ◆ GRATING
- ◆ SPREADING

1 Turn the grill on – you will need to ask an adult to show you how to do this, as all grills are different. Put the bagel halves, cut-side up, onto a baking tray. Tear the ham and put onto the bagel halves around the holes in the middle. Avoid the hole otherwise the ham will fall into it!

2 To grate the cheese, hold the handle of the grater with one hand and use the other hand to push the cheese downwards over the grater 'teeth'. Always keep your fingers away from the grater 'teeth', as they are very sharp. Sprinkle the cheese on the ham.

3 Ask an adult to help you put the tray under the grill using oven gloves. Grill for 3–4 minutes or until the cheese is golden and bubbling. Keep watching it – this will only take a few minutes and if you leave the bagel under the grill for too long it might burn. Ask an adult to help you take the tray from under the grill using oven gloves, and see how the cheese has melted!

4 Spread a little chutney over the top.

tropical smoothie

Pawpaws have a green skin that turns yellow as it ripens and the orange flesh is sweet. Passion fruits are small and dark, and their skin wrinkles when it ripens. The skin can be quite tough, so you may need to ask for help with cutting through it. Most smoothies are made using a blender, but they have a very sharp blade that cuts the fruit into tiny pieces, so ask an adult to help you when you use one.

To make 2 glasses you need:

INGREDIENTS
1 pawpaw
1 passion fruit
1 ripe banana
2 small glasses fresh orange juice

EQUIPMENT
chopping board ◆ small paring knife
spoon ◆ blender ◆ spoon ◆ 2 tall glasses

SKILLS
◆ USING BLENDER
◆ CHOPPING WITH PARING KNIFE

1 Use the bridge-cutting technique to cut the pawpaw in half lengthways: on a chopping board, make a 'bridge' with a thumb and finger of one hand and hold the pawpaw. Hold a small paring knife in your other hand and put the blade under the bridge, then cut downwards firmly. Cut the passion fruit in half in the same way. You might ask an adult or older child to help you, as passion fruits are quite tough. Using a spoon, scrape the black seeds out of the pawpaw and throw away.

2 Peel the banana, break it into 2 or 3 pieces and put into the blender. Using a teaspoon, scoop the orange pawpaw flesh into the blender, too. Now scrape the seeds and juice from the passion fruit on top of the pawpaw.

3 Pour the orange juice in the blender, put the lid on and blend until smooth. (Ask an adult or older child to help you.)

4 Pour the smoothie into 2 tall glasses.

STAGE
2

Finley's lemonberryade

Finley likes to make this when we have friends round. The lemonade without the raspberries will keep for at least a week in a bottle in the fridge. If you do add raspberries, only add them when you are ready to drink the lemonade.

SKILLS

CHOPPING WITH PARING KNIFE
SQUEEZING LEMONS ◆ POURING
MEASURING LIQUIDS ◆ MASHING
USING SIEVE

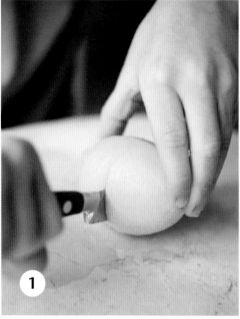

1 You might like to ask an adult to help you with this, as lemons are quite tough to cut. Use the bridge-cutting technique to cut the lemons: on a chopping board, make a 'bridge' with a thumb and finger of one hand and hold the lemon. Hold a small paring knife in your other hand and put the blade under the bridge, then cut downwards firmly.

2 Put a lemon half over a lemon juicer and press down. Try to turn the lemon as you press down. If you don't have a lemon juicer, you might like to try cutting the lemon half in half again using the bridge-cutting technique to make quarters and then squeeze the lemon quarters with your hands.

3 Before you pour the juice into a nice jug, if there are any pips in the juice, pour it through a sieve into the jug so that the sieve catches the pips.

4 Add the sugar to the jug and stir with a big spoon until the sugar has dissolved (or disappeared).

5 Pour cold water into a measuring jug up to the 1-litre mark. Pour the water into the lemon juice.

6 When you are ready to drink the lemonberryade, put the raspberries in a bowl and mash them with a fork. Add them to the lemonade and stir. You need to sieve the lemonade again into another jug, pushing the raspberries though the sieve with a fork as you go.

5

To make 8 glasses you need:

INGREDIENTS
4 lemons
130 g golden caster sugar
1 litre cold water
handful fresh raspberries
ice cubes, if you want to make
the drink cold!

EQUIPMENT
*chopping board ◆ small paring
knife ◆ lemon juicer ◆ small sieve
nice jug ◆ big spoon ◆ measuring
jug ◆ small bowl ◆ fork*

6

Tips: If you are going to drink this
lemonade as soon as you have made it,
you could try using sparkling water to make
it fizzy!

And now that you know how to juice fruit,
you might like to make some freshly
squeezed orange juice for breakfast.

STAGE
2

flower & herb ice bowl

I first made one of these in my home economics (now called design technology) lessons at school and I still remember how cool I thought it was to have made my own bowl. You could scoop your favourite ice cream or sorbet into the middle, or just put fresh summer fruits inside. Whatever you choose, I bet your friends will be impressed with the bowl. Remember, you will need to be patient and wait several hours until this is frozen.

To make 1 beautiful ice bowl you need:

INGREDIENTS
fresh edible flowers and/or fresh herbs or any pretty leaves from the garden (we used pink rose petals, rosemary, thyme and sage)

You might like to fill your bowl with a yoghurt and fruit mix like the berry crunch on page 40, but you will need to make more to fill your ice bowl (without the cereal). You will also need lots of fresh raspberries and strawberries.

EQUIPMENT
big freezerproof bowl ◆ small freezerproof bowl ◆ small weight ◆ sticky tape ◆ clean tea towel ◆ plate

1 Take your 2 bowls and pour enough cold water into the big bowl to half fill it. Scatter some fresh flowers and/or herbs in the water.

2 Rest the small bowl inside the big bowl and put a small weight in the small bowl to help it sit still. Stretch sticky tape across the tops of the bowls in several directions to hold the small bowl in place inside the big bowl. Put in the freezer and leave overnight.

3 The next day, peel off the sticky tape and carefully pull the small bowl out of the big bowl.

4 Lay a clean tea towel on the work surface and tip the big bowl upside down to let the ice bowl slip out. Turn the ice bowl the right way up and sit it on a plate. Fill your ice bowl with the yoghurt and fruit mix and top with fresh raspberries and strawberries.

Tip: You might need to sit the big bowl in a little warm water to help ease the ice bowl out of it, but don't leave it sitting in warm water for long otherwise it will melt.

SKILLS
- FREEZING
- PICKING FRESH HERBS

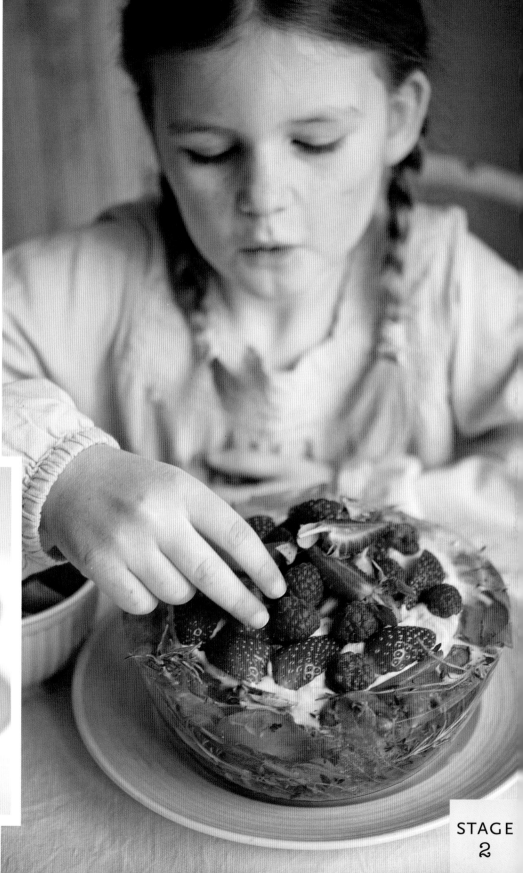

fruit & seed bread loaf

This is easy – you mix the wet ingredients together, then pour them into the dry ingredients. This is half like a cake and half like bread, but you don't need yeast like you do for bread. Look at page 88 for how to make pizza dough using yeast.

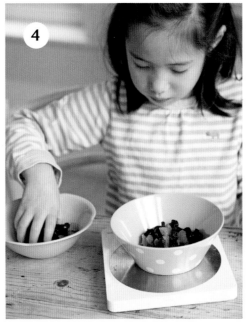

To make 2 small loaves you need:

INGREDIENTS
a little unsalted butter
300 ml natural yoghurt (not a thick-set yoghurt)
2 free-range eggs
3 tablespoons sunflower oil
capful vanilla extract
100 g dried fruit e.g. dried cranberries, raisins or chopped apricots or a mixture of all 3
150 g chopped nuts, seeds or desiccated coconut or a mixture of all 3
250 g self-raising flour
125 g golden caster sugar
1 teaspoon baking powder

EQUIPMENT
greaseproof paper ◆ 2 x 500-g loaf tins scissors ◆ table knife ◆ small bowl ◆ spoon fork ◆ measuring jug ◆ mixing bowl wooden spoon ◆ oven gloves ◆ skewer

1 Turn the oven on to 180°C (350°F) Gas 4. Using a scrap of greaseproof paper, rub a little butter inside the loaf tins. Now using scissors, cut a piece of greaseproof paper to fit along the bottom of the tins and up the ends. Fit it inside the tins – this will make it really easy to pull the bread out after it's baked.

2 Spoon the natural yoghurt into a measuring jug and stop when it reaches the 300-ml mark on the jug.

3 Crack open the eggs: hold an egg in one hand and carefully use a table knife to crack the egg in the middle. Put your thumbs into the crack and pull the egg shell apart. Let the egg fall into a bowl. Repeat with the other egg. Fish out any egg shell with a spoon. (See page 60 for a photo of how to crack eggs.) Mix with a fork. Add the eggs,

5

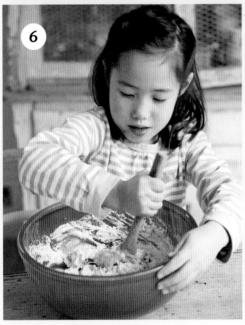

6

SKILLS
- ◆ GREASING
- ◆ POURING
- ◆ WEIGHING
- ◆ MEASURING
- ◆ MIXING
- ◆ DIVIDING
- ◆ USING OVEN

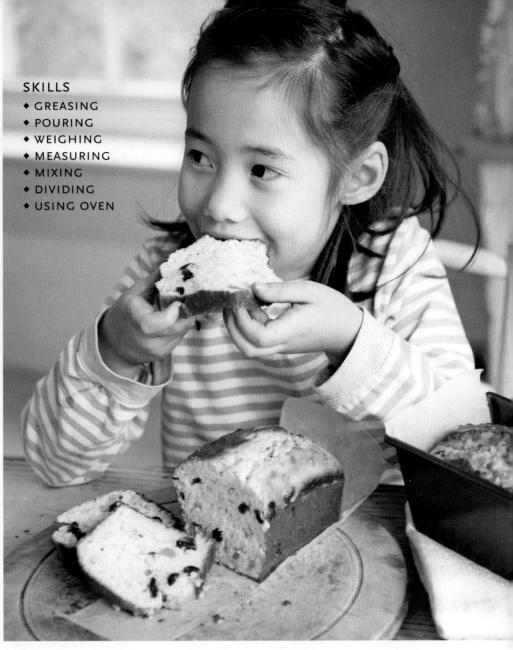

sunflower oil and vanilla to the yoghurt and mix with a fork.

4 Weigh the dried fruit, nuts, flour and sugar. How you weigh them will depend on the weighing scales you use. (See pages 50 and 52 for more information about how to weigh ingredients.)

5 Put all the weighed dry ingredients – dried fruit, nuts, flour and sugar – into a

mixing bowl. Add the baking powder and mix together. Pour the yoghurt mixture into the mixing bowl, too.

6 Use the wooden spoon to mix everything together. Spoon half the mixture into one loaf tin and the other half into the other tin. Ask an adult to help you put the loaf tins in the oven using oven gloves. Bake for about

30 minutes, or until golden and risen. Ask an adult to help you test if the loaves are cooked by poking the middle with a skewer – it should come out clean. Leave the loaves to cool down until they're cool enough to touch. Pull the ends of the greaseproof paper up at each end of the loaf tins and pull the bread out.

STAGE
2

shortbread shapes

If ever my children want to bake and we don't seem to have much in the cupboard, this is what they make. When you choose your cutters for making the shortbread shapes, make sure they are roughly the same size, because if you put big shortbreads onto a tray with little shortbreads, the little shortbreads will be cooked a long time before the big ones! This recipe makes a lot of shapes – the number will depend on the size of the cutters that you choose.

To make lots of shortbread shapes you need:

INGREDIENTS
125 g unsalted butter – soft
55 g golden caster sugar plus a little extra
1 capful vanilla extract
175 g plain flour
1 tablespoon milk

EQUIPMENT
scissors ◆ greaseproof paper

baking tray ◆ mixing bowl
wooden spoon ◆ rolling pin
pound coin ◆ shaped cutters
fork ◆ oven gloves

SKILLS
◆ LINING TRAYS
◆ CREAMING
◆ ROLLING
◆ CUTTING
◆ USING OVEN

1 Turn the oven on to 190°C (375°F) Gas 5. Cut a piece of greaseproof paper big enough to cover the baking tray.
2 Put the soft butter, sugar and vanilla extract in a mixing bowl and mix well with a wooden spoon until it becomes fluffy and paler in colour. This helps to beat air into the mixture.
3 Add the flour and milk to the bowl and mix until the mixture comes together to form a ball. You can do this with your hands or the wooden spoon.
4 Break the dough into 3 pieces. Sprinkle a little flour over the work surface and the rolling pin. Flatten one piece of dough

with a rolling pin until it is about the same thickness as a pound coin. Take the cutters you have chosen and, starting at the edge of the dough, push them down into the dough to cut out shapes. Repeat with the rest of the dough pieces.
5 Carefully lift the shapes onto the baking tray, then press a fork gently onto the shortbread to make pretty patterns. Sprinkle a little sugar over the top of the shortbread. Ask an adult to help you put the tray in the oven using oven gloves. Bake for 10 minutes (if they are small shapes) or 15 minutes (if they are big shapes), or until golden.

what's-in-season fruit crumble

One of the first things my mum taught me to make was a crumble. It's a great way to learn how to rub butter into flour. Once you know how to do this you can have a go at making pastry (see page 114). You can sprinkle this crumble mix on top of so many different fruits. Try to choose fruit that is in season – if you are not sure what that is, ask your greengrocer or the person who works in the fruit section of the supermarket. Fresh or frozen berries are easy to use as you don't need to chop them first.

1 Turn the oven on to 180°C (350°F) Gas 4. To make the fruit filling, use the bridge-cutting technique to cut the plums in half: on a chopping board, make a 'bridge' with a thumb and finger of one hand and hold the plum. Hold a small paring knife in your other hand and put the blade under the bridge, then cut downwards firmly. Move the plums around as you cut to avoid cutting through the stone. Take out the stones.
2 Put the plums into 2 small or 1 large ovenproof dish. Pour the orange juice over the plums, add the sugar and flour and mix with a spoon or your hands.

3 To make the crumble topping, put the flour into a bowl, add the butter and rub the butter into the flour with your fingers until it looks like fine breadcrumbs (see page 114 for photos showing you how to do this). This can take a few minutes. Add the oats, sugar and spice and mix with your fingers again.
4 Spoon the mixture over the top of the plums. Ask an adult to help you put the dishes into the oven using oven gloves. Bake for 25–30 minutes, or until the crumble topping is crisp, the plums are soft and the fruit juices are bubbling up around the edges.

STAGE
2

SKILLS
- ◆ RUBBING IN
- ◆ CUTTING WITH KNIFE
- ◆ MIXING WITH SPOON
- ◆ SPRINKLING TOPPING

For 4–6 people you need:

FRUIT FILLING
seasonal fruit e.g. 15 plums or about
600 g fresh or frozen berries or about
12 peaches or nectarines
4 tablespoons orange juice
3 tablespoons light brown soft sugar
1 level tablespoon plain flour

CRUMBLE TOPPING
150 g plain flour
100 g unsalted butter – chilled and cut
into small pieces
2 handfuls oats (or muesli if you prefer)
4 tablespoons light brown soft sugar
1 teaspoon ground mixed spice or
cinnamon

EQUIPMENT
chopping board ◆ small paring knife
spoon ◆ 2 small or 1 large ovenproof dish

Ella's marshmallow & chocolate squares

Ella made this recipe up one day when she found some chocolate and marshmallows in the cupboard. She asked me how much butter and syrup to add and then she did the rest! This is only to be eaten occasionally, as it is very, very sweet! Remember, you will need to be patient while you wait for it to set.

To make about 30 small pieces you need:

INGREDIENTS
12 biscuits e.g. Digestives, Rich Tea or Ginger Nuts
50 g mini-marshmallows
150 g dried fruit e.g. raisins, chopped mango, chopped apricots
100 g milk chocolate
100 g unsalted butter, chopped into big chunks
5 tablespoons golden syrup

EQUIPMENT
mixing bowl • large saucepan teaspoon • wooden spoon greaseproof paper • any cake tin (round, square or loaf tin) scissors • table knife

SKILLS
◆ MELTING CHOCOLATE
◆ MIXING
◆ SETTING IN FRIDGE

1 Using a scrap of greaseproof paper, rub a little butter inside the cake tin. Now using scissors, cut a piece of greaseproof to fit along the bottom of the tin and up the ends. Fit it inside the tin. Put the biscuits into a mixing bowl. Break them into small pieces. Add the mini-marshmallows and dried fruit.
2 Break the chocolate into small pieces and put into a large saucepan with the butter. Add the golden syrup – you might need to use a teaspoon to scrape the syrup off the tablespoon.
3 Ask an adult to help you turn the hob onto low heat and put the pan over it. Leave for a few minutes until the chocolate starts to melt. Stir everything with a wooden spoon until it's smooth. Take the pan off the heat, add the fruit mixture and stir everything together.
4 Spoon the mixture into the tin and push it down with the spoon. Cover with greaseproof paper and put in the fridge for 4 hours or until hard. Pull the ends of the greaseproof paper up at each end of the tin and pull the mixture out – you may need to run a table knife along the sides to help release it from the tin. Cut into small pieces and put into a jar.

4

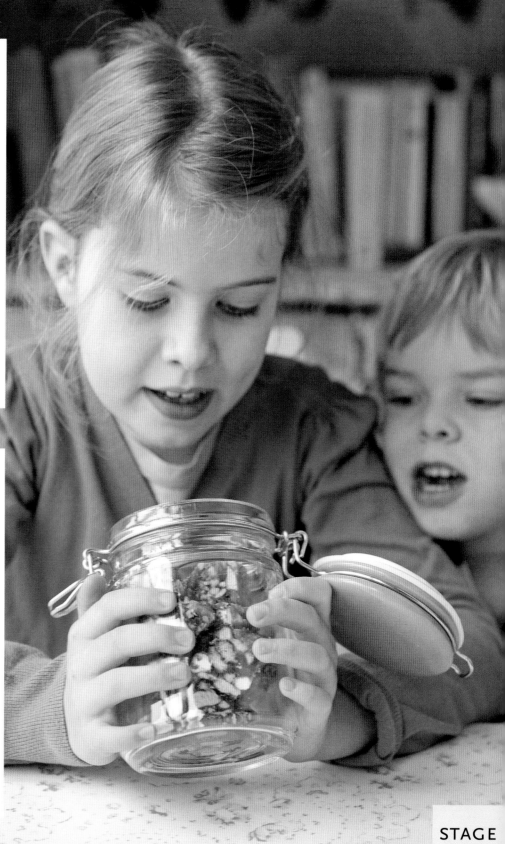

bumblebee cakes

Have you ever made butterfly cakes? My children and their friends have made a variation of the butterfly cake, the bumblebee. It's flavoured with orange, but you could just add vanilla if you prefer. Make them plain or with cocoa powder.

To make 10 bumblebee cakes you need:

CAKES
½ orange
125 g unsalted butter – soft
125 g golden caster sugar
capful vanilla extract
2 free-range eggs
125 g self-raising flour OR if you want to make them chocolatey use 100 g self-raising flour and 25 g cocoa powder

BUTTERCREAM
½ orange
50 g unsalted butter – soft
125 g icing sugar

TO DECORATE
chocolate buttons and chocolate matchsticks (or long thin sweets)

EQUIPMENT
mixing bowl ◆ wooden spoon ◆ table knife 2 bowls ◆ large metal spoon ◆ 12-hole fairy cake tin lined with 12 fairy cake cases

1 Turn the oven on to 180°C (350°F) Gas 4. To make the cakes, squeeze the juice from the orange half into a mixing bowl and add the soft butter, sugar and vanilla extract. Mix well with a wooden spoon until it becomes fluffy and paler in colour. This helps to beat air into the mixture. Now you need to crack open the eggs: hold an egg in one hand and carefully use a table knife to crack the egg in the middle. Put your thumbs into the crack and pull the egg shell apart. Let the egg fall into a bowl. Repeat with the other egg. Fish out any egg shell with a spoon. (See page 58 for a photo of how to crack eggs.)
2 Add the eggs to the butter mixture and beat. Add the flour and 'fold' in (see page 51) with a metal spoon.
3 Divide the mixture evenly between the fairy cake cases with a spoon. Ask

an adult to help you put the tin in the oven using oven gloves. Bake for 12–15 minutes until golden and slightly springy when you touch them. Ask an adult to help you take the tin out of the oven using oven gloves and leave to cool.

4 Using a table knife, cut a small oval shape from the middle of each cake.

Cut this oval in half to make 2 wings.

5 To make the buttercream, squeeze the orange half into a bowl. Add the soft butter and sugar and mix well.

6 Spoon this into the holes in each cake, then stick the wings into the buttercream. Stick chocolate buttons and matchsticks into the cakes to make them look like bumblebees.

STAGE
2

Grown-ups: this page is for you

CHILDREN: YOU CAN SKIP THIS BIT AND HAVE FUN COOKING!

This age range is huge. Some children will be able to cook independently and others will still need some assistance. But here are a few things that your child will be beginning to do during this stage. Remind your child that she can go back to Stage 1 of the book as she will find those recipes easy to make.

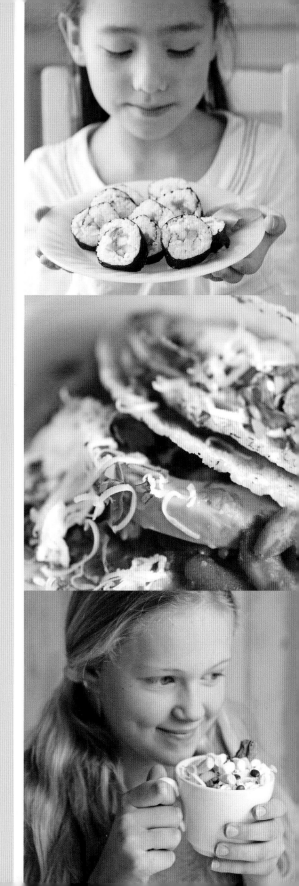

• It is likely that your child will be well into the swing of following the recipes on her own by now, and will be gaining independence and confidence in the kitchen. This is what this book is all about!

• She will enjoy the chance to try new pieces of kitchen equipment. Try to stand back and let her feel that she is in control, at the same time being nearby if help is needed. It is very easy to take over in the kitchen, so try to hold back.

• By now, most children like to cook with a friend or sibling. The sooner children realize that cooking is a fun and sociable activity, the better!

• She will have an increased ability to remember and should be able to easily repeat skills from the previous chapters. These new skills will be with her now for life.

• Her coordination will be greatly improved and she will have more control over smaller muscles, making it easier to complete more intricate tasks.

• She will be able to plan ahead more easily, for example if she is helping to make a meal, she will have a better understanding of timing and planning.

• She is likely to be keen to understand more about the science behind food, for example about yeast and kneading, and about cake making.

• Children at this age still enjoy learning through play, which is one reason why cooking is so great, as she can learn essential life skills while having fun in the kitchen.

• She will be able to start to teach other family members her new-found skills.

• Some children will be ready to cook a two- or even three-course meal for the family using the recipes from all the stages in this book – enjoy being cooked for!

• Make sure she helps to clear up after she has finished cooking! This is a really important life skill.

SKILLS

Here are more skills that you can learn and practise as you make the recipes in this chapter. You will also be using some skills from the previous chapters, but they will be so easy by now that you probably won't even realize you are using them.

PEELING VEGETABLES

Hold the fruit or vegetable in one hand and the peeler in the other hand. Press it onto the fruit or vegetable and push away from you. It is a good idea to practise peeling vegetables with different peelers to see which you find the easiest; there are lots of different kinds and some are easier to use than others.

KNEADING DOUGH

This means to bash and push the dough. This helps to move the yeast cells around the dough and makes it stretchy. You may need to knead for 10 minutes before the dough is ready. It should be smooth, stretchy and almost silky when you touch it. To test if the dough has been kneaded for long enough, roll it into a ball and prod it with your finger – it should spring back quickly.

MAKING A WHITE SAUCE

This is a great skill to learn, as once you know how to make a white sauce, you can then make a pasta meal for your family like the swirly pasta with leek, broccoli & cheese sauce on page 96. The best method is to make a 'roux', which is when you melt the butter in the pan, add the flour and then cook the flour and butter mixture to make a paste or 'roux'. You then add the milk to the paste and keep cooking. However, you can also try putting all the ingredients into the pan together. Use a balloon whisk to keep stirring the mixture over gentle heat until you have a smooth sauce. This is the 'all in one' method.

COOKING BASMATI RICE

This type of rice grows in India. You always want to use twice as much volume of water as rice. This means that if you want to cook 1 mug of rice, you will need 2 mugs of water. Put the rice and water into a saucepan and cover with the lid. Bring to the boil and then lower the heat under the hob until the rice is simmering. Cook for 14 minutes, then very carefully take the pan off the heat and stand it on a pan stand for 10 minutes. You should have white, fluffy rice at the end.

ROLLING UP SUSHI

This is great fun and gets easier the more you practise. Gently roll the seaweed around the rice and filling and gently press together.

LADLING

Sometimes it is easiest to use a ladle to transfer food like stew or soup from one container to another. A ladle is like a small bowl with a handle.

BASHING GARLIC

If you don't have a garlic crusher or if you prefer to keep the garlic clove whole – like for the lemony chicken recipe on page 110 – you can always just squash the garlic slightly to release some of its juices and flavour and keep it whole. Bash the clove of garlic with the end of a rolling pin to loosen the papery skin. Peel off the skin and throw away. Now bash the clove again with the end of the rolling pin to split the garlic slightly. Remember to wash the rolling pin.

BAKING JACKET POTATOES

Always prick the potatoes with a fork first and bake them in a very hot oven so that the skins are crisp and the insides are soft and fluffy.

SEPARATING EGGS

This is when you want to separate the yolks and the whites in the eggs. There are different ways to do this. For example, take 2 bowls. Crack the egg over one bowl and then carefully tip the white and yolk from one shell half into the other. As you move the egg between the shells, let the white gradually drop into the bowl until you're just left with the yolk in the egg shell. Now drop the yolk into the second bowl. Alternatively, you may prefer to crack the egg onto a saucer and then cover the yolk with a small bowl. Tip the saucer so that the white drips into a bowl, leaving the yolk behind on the saucer.

ROASTING

To roast something in the oven means to cook it at a high temperature with only a little fat, like olive oil.

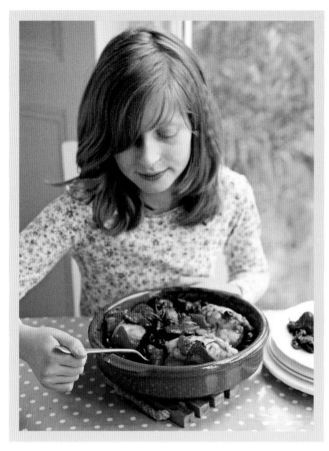

cook it. The marinade will help to keep the meat or fish juicy as it cooks.

WHISKING EGG WHITES
If you are using a balloon whisk to whisk egg whites, you might need to pass the whisk to a friend and take it in turns to stop your wrist from aching. If you use an electric whisk, it is much quicker!

WHY DO CAKES RISE?
When you beat together the butter and sugar and then beat in the eggs, you are adding air to the mixture. When you bake the cake, the air inside the bubbles gets bigger, helping the cake to rise. Many cakes use self-raising flour and sometimes baking powder too. These both contain carbon dioxide, which is released as a gas when it is heated. As the carbon dioxide becomes a gas, it gets bigger and pushes the cake up, making it rise.

MELTING CHOCOLATE
Find a small bowl that will sit on top of a saucepan so that the bottom of the bowl is just under the rim of the pan. Break the chocolate into small pieces (this helps it to melt quickly and evenly) and put into the small bowl. Half fill the saucepan with water, put the bowl of chocolate on top and bring it to a gentle simmer. Leave for a few minutes, then turn the heat off. Stir the chocolate carefully until it has melted. If the chocolate gets too hot, the cocoa butter will begin to separate from the cocoa solids, and the chocolate can become dry and crumbly. It is really important that you do not let any liquid like water drip into the chocolate – even a tiny amount can cause the chocolate to harden and turn into a solid lump! If this happens you will need to start again.

LAYING A TABLE FOR A MEAL
If you are serving a starter as well as a main course, you will need to lay two sets of cutlery at the table. Put the knife and fork on the table as normal and then lay a smaller knife and fork on the outside of this cutlery for the starter. When you eat a meal with more than one course, start with the cutlery on the outside and work your way into the middle.

COOKING PASTA
You will need the biggest pan that you can find so that the pasta has plenty of room to move around in the water as it cooks. This will help to make sure that it cooks evenly. See page 94 for more information about how to cook pasta.

DRAINING
You will need an adult or older child to help you drain pasta, as the saucepan will be heavy and the water will be very hot. Try to wear oven gloves to help prevent the water from splashing on your hands. Rest the colander in the sink and then very carefully pour the pasta and hot water into the colander.

MARINATING
A marinade can be made from a variety of ingredients, but it often contains an acid like lemon juice and an oil, plus a few other ingredients to add flavour. Add the meat or fish and leave to marinate for a little while to make sure that the flavours soak into the food before you

KITCHEN EQUIPMENT

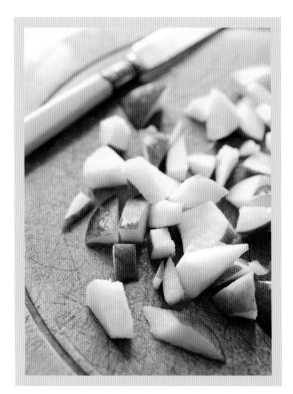

You have already used most of the basic kitchen utensils, but there are just a few other utensils that are worth mentioning in case you choose to cook all the recipes in this chapter.

WHISKS
You will need either a balloon whisk or an electric whisk to whisk egg whites until they are white and fluffy. I always recommend that if possible you have a go at whisking with a balloon whisk to practise how to whisk. You can always use an electric whisk later to see the difference.

SMALL PUDDING BASINS
These are good to have for making small puddings or you could use them for setting jellies. You might also hear an adult suggest that you use ramekins. These are small dishes that can be put into the oven.

VEGETABLE PEELER
These can be quite tricky to use, so you may need to have a go with friends' peelers until you find one that you are happy with.

SMALL GRATER
Some big graters have small holes on them that you can use for grating ingredients that you want to make tiny pieces from. If your big grater doesn't have small enough holes, you will need a small grater.

PAN STAND
As it sounds, this is a small stand for resting hot pans on. It is very handy to have a pan stand by your hob. You can then take something out of the oven or off the hob and put it on the pan stand. Never put anything hot onto the kitchen work surface, as you might damage the surface.

PASTA PAN
A pasta pan has its own colander inside the pan, ready for draining the pasta when it is cooked. Most Italians have a pasta pan, as they like to cook pasta a lot. It doesn't matter if you don't have one – just use a large pan and a colander instead. (Always ask an adult to drain the pasta for you, as the pan will be heavy and full of boiling water.)

ROASTING DISH
Ideally you need a heavy-based roasting dish. This will heat up and cook the food without burning it.

WOK OR LARGE FRYING PAN
Now that you are used to cooking on the hob, you might like to try making the stir-fry on page 92. The best pan for a stir-fry is a wok, as it is large enough to give you space to toss the vegetables around and 'stir' them as you 'fry'. If you don't have a wok, you could use a large frying pan instead.

FLUTED CUTTERS
Some cook shops sell these individually, or you could buy a set so that you have different-sized cutters to play with.

12-HOLE FAIRY-CAKE TIN
This tin is ideal for making small cakes or tarts. Once you know how to make pastry, you can make up your own tart recipe.

2 x 20-CM SANDWICH TINS
If you only have one sandwich tin and you want to make a sandwich cake like a Victoria sponge where you sandwich 2 cakes together, you need to make half the mixture and bake it, then make the other half and bake it. Or you can see if a neighbour or friend has another cake tin you could use.

SUSHI MAT OR NAPKIN
You don't have to have a sushi mat to make sushi – you can use a napkin instead. A sushi mat is used to help roll the sushi into a long sausage shape.

BOWLS FOR MARINATING
When you marinate fish, meat or vegetables, put the marinade ingredients in a glass, Pyrex, melamine or plastic bowl, not a metal one. Acidic ingredients like lemon juice and vinegar can react with the metal and give the food a funny taste.

ham & pineapple pizzas

We often have these on a Saturday night. They are fun to make and cheaper than going out for pizza in a restaurant. Did you know that yeast is alive? It is a living micro-organism used to make bread rise and give it a lighter, more open texture. For the yeast to work, it needs to grow (or reproduce). To do this it needs warmth (from warm water), moisture (water), and food (sugar from the flour). The yeast produces a gas, carbon dioxide, which makes the bread rise before it is baked. We bake pizzas in a very hot oven to kill the yeast so that they don't carry on rising.

1 Put the flour into a mixing bowl. Sprinkle the yeast over the top.

2 Make a well (a hole) in the middle of the flour with your hand. Pour the warm water into a measuring jug up to the 200-ml mark. Make sure the water is warm and not too hot — when you put your finger in, it should feel just warm. Add the olive oil to the water, then pour into the well. Use a wooden spoon to stir the liquid, and the flour will gradually fall into the water. Keep stirring until all the flour has mixed with the liquid and you have a dough.

3 Sprinkle a little flour over the work surface, take the dough out of the bowl and knead the dough. The best way to knead is to push the dough down and away with the heel of the hand and then pull it back with your fingers. Push it back onto the work surface, turn the dough slightly and then repeat. After a few minutes of doing this, the dough should have a smooth, elastic texture.

4 Clean the mixing bowl and put the dough back in. Now cover it with clingfilm or a clean tea towel and leave it somewhere warm to rise for about an hour, or until it is twice as big — look how much the dough has grown!

5 Turn the oven on to 200°C (400°F) Gas 6. Dip a pastry brush into a little olive oil and brush it all over the baking sheets. Break the risen dough in half and, using a rolling pin, roll each piece into two large flat circles.

6 Lift the pizza bases onto the baking trays. Spread the tomato passata over the bases with the back of a spoon.

7 Scatter your ham and pineapple over the passata. Using oven gloves, put the trays in the oven and bake for 15–20 minutes or until the bases are cooked.

To make 2 very large or 3–4 small pizzas you need:

PIZZA DOUGH
350 g strong plain white flour
7-g packet 'easy bake' microfine yeast
2 tablespoons olive oil plus a little extra
200 ml warm (not hot) water

TOPPINGS
tomato passata, ham, pineapple, mozzarella and grated cheese OR tomato passata, prawns and sliced peppers OR any other topping combinations that you might like to try

EQUIPMENT
mixing bowl • measuring jug • wooden spoon • clingfilm • pastry brush 2 baking trays • rolling pin • spoon oven gloves

Did you know? Kneading the dough helps to distribute the yeast cells evenly and give the dough elasticity (which means it is stretchy). You may need to knead for up to 10 minutes before the dough is smooth, elastic and almost silky to touch. To test if the dough has been kneaded for long enough, roll it into a ball and prod it with your finger – it should spring back quickly.

SKILLS
◆ MAKING YEASTED DOUGH
◆ ROLLING
◆ SPREADING
◆ USING OVEN

tacos with soya beans & coriander

The mild chilli powder in this recipe gives the beans a slight chilli flavour, but you can always leave it out if you really don't like chilli – they will still taste good. This simple meal is as fun to make as it is to eat because there are lots of things to assemble, and so lots of things to try!

For 4 people you need:

INGREDIENTS
400 g tinned chopped tomatoes
2 x 400-g tins soya beans in water
(or cannellini beans)
2 spring onions
1 garlic clove
1 tablespoon olive oil
1 teaspoon ground coriander
1 teaspoon mild chilli powder
1 teaspoon golden caster sugar
handful fresh coriander leaves plus
a little extra
8–12 tacos
2 ripe avocados
150 ml soured cream
grated Cheddar cheese
pieces of lime

EQUIPMENT
*tin opener • colander • small paring
knife • chopping board • garlic crusher
small saucepan • wooden spoon
baking tray • oven gloves • spoon*

SKILLS
OPENING TINS • CUTTING
CRUSHING GARLIC
USING HOB • USING OVEN

1 Turn the oven on to 180°C (350°F) Gas 4. Use a tin opener to open the tins of tomatoes and soya beans. The first time you do this you will need an adult to show you how to use your tin opener, as they are all slightly different. Drain the beans in a colander.

2 Using the claw-cutting technique (see page 50), cut the ends off the spring onions with a small paring knife and throw away. Cut the onions into thin slices.

3 Peel the garlic clove and crush it with a garlic crusher.

4 Put the oil and onions into a small saucepan over low heat on the hob. Heat gently, stirring every now and then with a wooden spoon, until they are soft. This will take about 5 minutes. Add the crushed garlic, ground coriander and chilli powder and cook for another minute.

5 Add the tinned tomatoes, drained beans, sugar and coriander leaves. Turn the heat up, and when the

tomatoes are bubbling, lower the heat and leave to simmer gently for 10 minutes.

6 Put the tacos on a baking tray and, using oven gloves, put them in the oven for 3 minutes to heat up. Scoop the stones out of the avocados with a teaspoon and peel away the skins. Using the claw-cutting technique, cut the avocados into slices. Put the beans, soured cream, cheese, extra coriander, avocado and lime in bowls. Let everyone make their own tacos.

STAGE
3

rainbow stir-fry

I have used ready-prepared vegetables here so that all you need to prepare are the leeks and green beans, but when you have practised using a small sharp knife, you may like to add other vegetables like sliced red or yellow peppers or pak choi.

For 4 people you need:

INGREDIENTS

1 leek, trimmed and washed
200 g green beans
2 large handfuls fresh coriander leaves
2 garlic cloves
small piece ginger, about 2 cm
2 teaspoons sesame oil
2 teaspoons olive oil
about 300 g crunchy vegetable stir-fry mix (pack sizes will vary; the amount doesn't have to be exact)
300 g pre-cooked free-range egg noodles
2 large handfuls pine nuts or peanuts, if you like
1–2 tablespoons low-salt soy sauce

EQUIPMENT

small paring knife • chopping board
scissors • garlic crusher • small grater
wok or large frying pan • wooden spoon

1 Use the bridge-cutting technique to cut the leeks in half widthways, then lengthways with a small paring knife. Using the claw-cutting technique, thinly slice the leeks.
2 Using scissors, snip the coriander into small pieces. Still using scissors, cut the ends off the beans and throw them away. Cut the beans in half.
3 Peel the garlic clove and crush it with a garlic crusher. Grate the ginger using a small grater (you don't need to peel it first).
4 Turn the hob onto medium heat. Heat the oils in a wok or large frying pan. Add the leeks and fry for a few minutes, stirring with a wooden spoon. Add the garlic, ginger and beans and fry for another minute.
5 Add the vegetable stir-fry mix and fry for another minute. Add the noodles, coriander, nuts and soy sauce and fry for a few minutes, stirring as you fry.

SKILLS
- KNIFE SKILLS
- STIR-FRYING
- GRATING
- CRUSHING GARLIC
- PREPARING VEGETABLES

how to cook pasta

Knowing how to cook pasta is a great skill, as it is so easy to make it into a lovely meal. However, you will need help from an adult, as the pasta pan will be very heavy and full of hot water!

For 1 person you need:
INGREDIENTS
75–115 g dried pasta

EQUIPMENT
the biggest saucepan you can find • jug • long-handled or wooden spoon

a Ideally you need 1 litre of water for every 100 g pasta, but this will only work if you have a pan big enough for this amount of water. However, only ever three-quarters fill your saucepan. Don't fill it to the top or it will overflow when you add the pasta!

b Find the biggest saucepan that you have in your kitchen (the pasta needs to be cooked in a large pan to help make sure that it cooks evenly; if the pan is too small, some of the pasta may be trapped at the bottom of the pan and it will cook more quickly than the pasta at the top). Turn the hob onto medium heat and put the pan of water on it. Heat the water until it comes to the boil – you will know that it is boiling when you can see the water bubbling.

c Put your pasta into a jug and then carefully add the pasta to the water (keep your hands away from the hot water!) Using a long-handled spoon, gently swirl the pasta around in the pan to help stop it from sticking together. Bring the water back to the boil and cook following the packet instructions (all pastas have different cooking times). Use a fork to take a piece of pasta from the pan, leave to cool slightly and then test to see if it is ready: when you bite into it, it should be cooked but still have a little 'bite' – this is known as 'al dente' in Italy. When it is cooked, put a colander in the sink and ask an adult to pour the pasta into the colander for you (remember, the pan will be very heavy) to drain it.

pasta sauces

pepper pasta sauce

You need to use just plain roasted peppers for this recipe, not antipasti peppers that have lots of oils and herbs added to them.

For 4 people you need:

INGREDIENTS
300 g roasted red peppers from a jar
300 g pasta shapes, cooked and drained (see opposite for instructions)
handful fresh basil or coriander leaves
handful baby spinach leaves
4 tablespoons cream cheese

EQUIPMENT
colander • scissors • saucepan wooden spoon

Drain the roasted peppers in a colander in the sink. Using scissors, snip the peppers into really small pieces (the smaller the better) and add to the cooked and drained pasta in the saucepan. Tear the basil or coriander leaves and spinach into small pieces and add to the pasta with the cream cheese. Put the pan over low heat and cook until the cream cheese has melted, stirring gently with a wooden spoon.

tuna pasta sauce

This is one of my daughter Lola's favourite quick suppers, and she also loves it cold in her packed lunchbox for school.

For 4 people you need:

INGREDIENTS
150 g tinned or frozen (and defrosted) sweetcorn
2 x 185-g tins tuna, drained
3–4 tablespoons mayonnaise
300 g pasta shapes, cooked and drained (see opposite for instructions)

EQUIPMENT
tin opener • colander • bowl fork • spoon

Use a tin opener to open the tin of sweetcorn. The first time you do this you will need an adult to show you how to use your tin opener, as they all differ slightly. If you are using frozen sweetcorn, you will need to leave it to defrost for at least 1 hour before you make the pasta sauce. Use the tin opener to open the tin of tuna. Drain both the sweetcorn and tuna in a colander, then tip into a bowl. Break the tuna up with a fork, add the mayonnaise and mix. Spoon the mixture over the cooked pasta and mix well.

STAGE
3

swirly pasta with leek, broccoli & cheese sauce

It's useful to know how to make a white sauce like this one because it is used in many dishes like lasagne, macaroni cheese, cauliflower cheese etc.

1 Turn the oven on to 190°C (375°F) Gas 5. Use the claw-cutting technique to cut the broccoli into chunks with a small paring knife. Using the same technique, slice the leek into thin slices.

2 Turn the hob onto low heat. Put the leek and butter into a saucepan on the hob and heat gently. Cook for about 10 minutes, or until the leek has softened. Stir with a wooden spoon. Add the flour.

3 Stir and cook for a few minutes until you have a thick paste. Now take a balloon whisk and, whisking all the time, slowly pour in the milk. Keep whisking until you have a smooth sauce and cook gently for a few minutes. Add the mustard and almost all the cheese (keep some for the top) to the sauce, stir and take off the heat.

4 Cook the pasta following the instructions on page 94. Add the broccoli to the pasta pan 2 minutes before the pasta has finished cooking. When it is cooked, put a colander in the sink and ask an adult to pour the pasta and broccoli into the colander for you. Tip the pasta and broccoli from the colander into an ovenproof dish. Pour the sauce over the top and sprinkle the last bit of cheese over it. Using oven gloves, put the dish in the oven. Cook for 25–30 minutes until the topping is golden and the sauce is bubbling.

For 4 people you need:

INGREDIENTS
300 g broccoli tender stems
1 leek, trimmed and washed
50 g unsalted butter
50 g plain flour
500 ml full-fat milk
1 teaspoon English mustard
2 large handfuls grated Cheddar cheese
250 g pasta spirals

EQUIPMENT
small paring knife • chopping board
saucepan • wooden spoon • balloon whisk
colander • ovenproof dish • oven gloves

SKILLS
◆ CHOPPING
◆ MAKING WHITE SAUCE
◆ COOKING PASTA
◆ USING OVEN

STAGE
3

easy minestrone soup

The great thing about this soup is that you don't have to blend it at the end of cooking. It's ready to eat just as it is, all lovely and chunky.

For 4 people you need:

INGREDIENTS
4 spring onions
1 garlic clove
1 tablespoon olive oil
500 g tomato passata
1 teaspoon sugar
390-g carton soya beans in water
100 g pasta for soup
2 large handfuls frozen peas
2 tablespoons pesto
handful grated Parmesan

EQUIPMENT
small paring knife • chopping board rolling pin • garlic crusher • heavy-based saucepan • wooden spoon

1 Using the claw-cutting technique, cut the ends off the spring onions with a small paring knife and throw away. Now slice the onions into thin slices.
2 Bash the garlic clove with a rolling pin, then peel off the skin.
3 Crush the garlic clove using a garlic crusher.
4 Turn the hob onto low heat. Heat the olive oil in a heavy-based saucepan on the hob and fry the onions and garlic for 2 minutes, stirring every now and then with a wooden spoon. Pour the passata into the pan. Fill the passata container with water and pour into the pan. Do this twice. Add the sugar.
5 Add the soya beans. Turn the heat up to high and cook until the mixture is simmering. Lower the heat and simmer gently for 15 minutes.
6 Add the pasta, peas and pesto and cook for another 5 minutes (or however long the packet of pasta says). Sprinkle the grated Parmesan on top.

Tip: To add green beans instead of peas, cut the ends off using scissors and compost them (or throw them away), then cut the beans into small pieces before you put them into the soup.

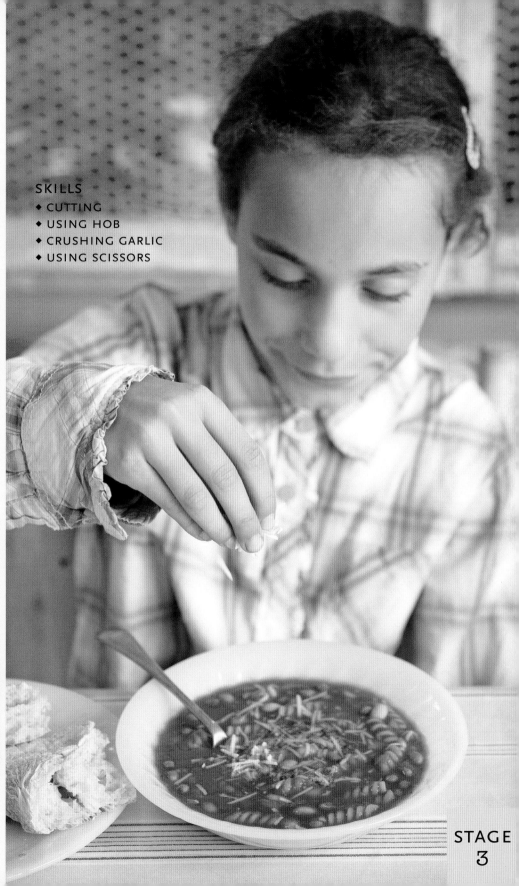

SKILLS
- ◆ CUTTING
- ◆ USING HOB
- ◆ CRUSHING GARLIC
- ◆ USING SCISSORS

5

6

STAGE
3

fish curry with rice

Have you ever been to a curry house? You may think that all curries are hot and spicy, but they are not. They can be mild and creamy and taste delicious like this.

For 4 people you need:

INGREDIENTS
big handful fresh coriander leaves
3 spring onions
1 tablespoon olive oil
3 tablespoons mild curry paste
400 g tinned chopped tomatoes
200 ml hot vegetable stock or hot water
large handful few different vegetables e.g. baby corn and green beans
300 g mixed fresh fish fillets e.g. haddock, salmon, monkfish, chopped into big chunks, or raw peeled prawns
cooked long-grain rice (see opposite for instructions)
naan bread, poppadoms and mango chutney, to serve

EQUIPMENT
scissors • small paring knife • chopping board • large saucepan • wooden spoon

1 Using scissors, snip the coriander into small pieces. Using the bridge-cutting technique, slice the vegetables in half lengthways with a small paring knife. Using the claw-cutting technique, cut the ends off the spring onions and throw away. Now cut the onions into thin slices. Turn the hob onto low heat. Put the onions and oil into a large saucepan on the hob and heat gently.
2 Add the curry paste and fry for a few minutes, stirring with a wooden spoon.
3 Add the tinned tomatoes to the pan, then fill the tin with the hot stock or water and add to the pan. Simmer for 10 minutes, stirring once or twice.
4 Add the vegetables and cook for 5 minutes. Add the fish and cook until the fish is cooked – this will only be 5 minutes, as you don't want to overcook it. Ask an adult to help you check if it is cooked. Add the snipped coriander and stir. Serve with cooked rice, naan, poppadoms and chutney.

SKILLS
- ◆ CHOPPING
- ◆ COOKING RICE
- ◆ SIMMERING
- ◆ USING HOB

how to cook rice

For 2 people you need:

INGREDIENTS
1 tall glass of long-grain rice

EQUIPMENT
tall glass • saucepan

a Measure 1 tall glass or cup of rice. Put the rice and then 2 glasses of water into a saucepan. Turn the hob onto medium heat and put the pan on the heat.

b Bring the water in the pan up to the boil, lower the heat, put the lid on and simmer for 14 minutes. Ask an adult to help you take the pan off the heat and leave for 10 minutes with the lid on. The rice will continue to steam and become fluffy. Don't take the lid off during this time – it is important that the lid stays on if you want fluffy rice.

super sushi rolls

This looks so impressive and yet it is easy and great fun to make. You will need to look for the ingredients in a good supermarket. Read the cooking instructions on the packet of sushi rice before you cook it, but my method below is how most sushi rice is cooked so it's likely to be similar.

1 To cook the rice, put the water and rice into a large saucepan over medium heat on the hob. Heat until the water comes to the boil – you will know that it is boiling when the water is bubbling. Cover the pan with the lid, lower the heat and simmer for 10 minutes. Take the pan off the heat and leave to stand for 15 minutes with the lid on. Spoon the rice into a mixing bowl. In a small bowl, mix together the vinegar, sugar and salt. Pour the vinegar dressing over the rice, mix together and leave to cool.

2 Put a sheet of nori seaweed on a sushi mat. Use your hands or a spoon to cover two-thirds of the seaweed with rice. Leave a strip along the end of the seaweed furthest from you without rice. Press the rice down so that it is quite flat and evenly spread out.

3 Put a few strips of avocado and some prawns along the middle.

4 Pick up the edge of the mat closest to you and roll up the seaweed and its filling into a big sausage. Use the mat to help you roll the seaweed neatly.

5 Squash the roll to make the sushi nice and compact, then unroll the mat. Do all this again with the remaining sheets of seaweed, rice and filling. Using the claw-cutting technique, cut each roll of sushi into 5 or 6 pieces with a small paring knife and serve with pickled ginger and soy sauce, if you like.

SKILLS
COOKING SUSHI RICE
ROLLING UP SUSHI ◆ CUTTING

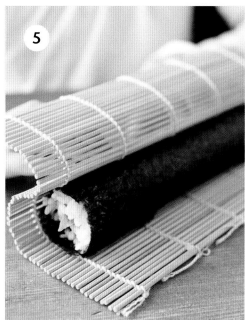

To make about 30 pieces you need:

RICE
450 ml water
225 g Japanese rice for sushi
2 tablespoons rice wine vinegar
1 tablespoon golden caster sugar
pinch salt
6 sheets nori seaweed

FILLINGS
ripe avocado strips and small, cooked prawns
OR smoked salmon and thin cucumber strips
OR try thin strips of omelette
You might like to eat your sushi with pickled
ginger and soy sauce

EQUIPMENT ◆ *large saucepan* ◆ *timer*
spoon ◆ *mixing bowl* ◆ *small bowl* ◆ *spoon*
sushi mat ◆ *small paring knife*

STAGE
3

Great granny's smoked haddock & spinach spuds

Have you ever baked a potato before? A good baked potato should have a crisp skin and a light, fluffy middle. To achieve this you will need to bake them for an hour in a hot oven. My granny taught me to make these when I was little. It was the first time I had ever cooked fish and I still remember how good it felt.

For 4 people you need:

INGREDIENTS
4 baking potatoes
3 smoked haddock fillets
a little unsalted butter
2 large handfuls baby spinach leaves
handful fresh herbs e.g. parsley or fennel tops
½ lemon
3 tablespoons crème fraîche or a little butter

EQUIPMENT
*fork • ovenproof dish • spoons • oven gloves
timer • scissors • mixing bowl • lemon juicer
fork • table knife • clean napkin • roasting dish*

1 Turn the oven on to 190°C (375°F) Gas 5. Prick the potatoes all over with a fork.

2 Put the smoked haddock into an ovenproof dish and dot with a little butter using teaspoons.

3 Using oven gloves, put the potatoes as well as the haddock into the oven. Set a timer for 15 minutes. Using oven gloves, take the haddock out of the oven and put to one side. Set the timer for 45 minutes more for the potatoes.

4 Using scissors, snip the herbs into small pieces and put into a mixing bowl. Tear the spinach into small pieces and put to one side. Squeeze the lemon half over a lemon juicer and pour the juice over the herbs. Add the crème fraîche. When the fish is cool enough to handle, peel the flesh away from the skin and flake the fish into the bowl. Mix everything together with a fork.

5 Using oven gloves, take the potatoes out of the oven. Leave to cool slightly. Holding a potato with a clean napkin or oven glove, use a table knife to cut the potato in half. Use a spoon to scoop the middle of the potato out of the potato skin and into the bowl with the haddock and herbs. Squash the chopped spinach into the potato skins. Mix the haddock mixture and cooked potato together in the bowl. Now spoon it back into the potato skins on top of the spinach. You will need to spoon the mixture between the potato skins. Using oven gloves, put the dish back in the oven and set the timer for another 10 minutes. Using oven gloves, take them out of the oven.

SKILLS
◆ USING SCISSORS
◆ BAKING POTATOES
◆ COOKING FISH
◆ SQUEEZING LEMONS
◆ USING OVEN
◆ SHARING

STAGE
3

beef & corn tortilla tubes

These are lots of fun to make and eat! The corn tortillas become all lovely and crisp when you bake them in the oven. (You will need to use corn tortillas, not flour ones). This is delicious with the green dip on page 30.

To make 8 tubes you need:

INGREDIENTS
1 red onion
1 garlic clove
3 carrots, well washed
1 tablespoon olive oil plus a little extra
500 g beef mince
500 g tomato passata
pinch brown sugar
8 corn tortillas
salad and Green Dip (page 30), to serve

EQUIPMENT
small paring knife • chopping board • garlic crusher • grater • frying pan • wooden spoon ovenproof dish • oven gloves

1 Turn the oven on to 190°C (375°F) Gas 5. Peel the onion. Use the bridge-cutting technique to halve it with a paring knife. Using the claw-cutting technique, thinly slice it. Peel the garlic clove and crush it with a garlic crusher. Grate the carrots with a grater.
2 Put the oil, onion, garlic and carrots into a heavy-based frying pan over low heat on the hob. Heat gently until soft.
3 Add the beef and fry for 10 minutes, or until the meat is turning golden brown. Add the passata and sugar, cover the pan with a lid and cook gently for 10 minutes. The mixture will be quite dry, which is what you want.
4 Lay the tortillas on the chopping board, then spoon some mince along the middle. Roll the tortillas around the mince and put into an ovenproof dish. Brush the tortilla tubes with a little oil. Using oven gloves, put the dish into the oven and cook for 15 minutes.

SKILLS ◆ **CUTTING** ◆ **CRUSHING GARLIC** ◆ **FRYING** ◆ **ROLLING USING OVEN**

all-in-one chicken

My girls really enjoy making a meal for the whole family to eat together, but they don't want to always spend long making it. This is why we came up with this recipe idea. To keep it really simple, put some baking potatoes into the oven to cook alongside the chicken. This is delicious with couscous (see page 62), rice (see page 101) or salad (see page 18).

For 4 people you need:

INGREDIENTS
185 g pitted black olives
300 g roasted red peppers from a jar
2 sprigs fresh rosemary
2 tablespoons olive oil
400 g tinned chopped tomatoes
2 garlic cloves
4 free-range chicken pieces e.g. thighs or legs
baked potatoes, rice or mashed potato, or bread and salad, to serve

EQUIPMENT
colander • scissors • mixing bowl • garlic crusher roasting dish • oven gloves

1 Turn the oven on to 180°C (350°F) Gas 4. Tip the olives (if they need draining) and peppers into a colander over a mixing bowl to drain. Now pour the liquid out of the bowl.

2 Using scissors, snip the peppers into small pieces and put into the dry mixing bowl.

3 Add the rosemary, olive oil and tinned tomatoes to the peppers and then squash the olives slightly to break them up and add to the bowl, too. Peel the garlic cloves and crush them with a garlic crusher. Add the crushed garlic to the bowl.

4 Pull the skin off the chicken, throw the skin away, then add the chicken to the bowl.

5 Mix everything with your hands to coat the chicken in the pepper and olive mixture. Now WASH YOUR HANDS. Tip everything into a roasting dish. Using oven gloves, put the dish in the oven and cook for 35–45 minutes (depending on the size of the chicken pieces), or until the chicken is cooked all the way through – ask an adult to help you check this.

SKILLS
◆ GARLIC CRUSHING
◆ USING SCISSORS
◆ USING OVEN

lemony chicken

To make a marinade, you normally mix together an acid, like lemon juice or vinegar with an oil, like olive oil, sunflower oil or sesame oil. You then add some flavour with chopped herbs, spices or garlic. The marinade helps to keep the food juicy and stops it from drying out during cooking. This is why people often make a marinade for meat before they cook it on a hot barbecue.

For 4 people you need:

INGREDIENTS
1 garlic clove
1 lemon
6 free-range skinless chicken thigh fillets
2 tablespoons olive oil
2 teaspoons honey
1 teaspoon dried oregano

EQUIPMENT
rolling pin ◆ chopping board ◆ small paring knife lemon juicer ◆ mixing bowl spoon ◆ roasting dish oven gloves

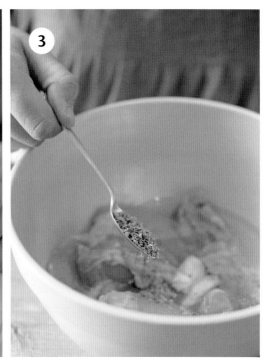

1 Bash the garlic clove with a rolling pin – this will help to loosen the pink papery skin – then peel off the skin. Using the rolling pin again, squash the garlic to crush it slightly – this helps its flavour to come out as it cooks. Remember to wash the rolling pin afterwards!

2 Use the bridge-cutting technique to halve the lemon with a small paring knife. Put a lemon half over a lemon juicer and press down to squeeze out the juice. Repeat with the other lemon half.

3 Put the chicken in a mixing bowl and add the garlic, lemon juice, oil, honey and dried oregano. Mix with a spoon, cover and put in the fridge for at least 1 hour. After 1 hour, turn the oven on to 190°C (375°F) Gas 5. Spoon the chicken into a roasting dish (leave the marinade behind). Using oven gloves, put the dish in the oven and roast for 25–30 minutes – ask an adult to help you check if it is cooked. Turn the chicken once during this time. Cut the chicken into small pieces to serve.

SKILLS
◆ BASHING GARLIC
◆ CUTTING
◆ MAKING MARINADE
◆ SQUEEZING LEMONS
◆ USING OVEN

STAGE
3

toffee apple tarts

These tarts are so enjoyable to make that the boys who came around to my house to make them for this book asked to make some more in between taking the photos. Once you know how to make pastry, you can make so many different pies, cheese straws, small tarts, big tarts and lots more.

1 Use a table knife to cut the butter into small pieces and put into a mixing bowl with the flour. Rub the butter into the flour with your fingers until it looks like fine breadcrumbs. This can take a few minutes.

2 Add the sugar, egg yolk and water and stir the mixture together with the table knife until it comes together and you can form a ball with your hands. Wrap the pastry in a piece of clingfilm and put it in the fridge for 30 minutes – this will make it easier to roll out.

3 Turn the oven on to 180°C (350°F) Gas 4. Using a scrap of greaseproof paper, rub a little butter inside the holes in the fairy cake tins. Break the pastry into 4 pieces. Sprinkle a little flour on the work surface, then roll out one piece at a time. Dip the cutter in flour, then cut out 24 circles. Gently press the circles into the holes of the tins.

4 Use the table knife and a chopping board to cut the apples in small pieces, avoiding the core in the middle. Divide the pieces between the pastry cases.

5 Put the toffees on a solid work surface and GENTLY bash with the rolling pin to break into pieces. Scatter the pieces evenly over the apples. Using oven gloves, put the tins in the oven and bake for 15 minutes, or until the toffee has melted and the apples are cooked.

5

To make 24 little tarts you need:

SWEET SHORTCRUST PASTRY
115 g unsalted butter – chilled
225 g plain flour
1 teaspoon golden caster sugar
1 egg yolk (see page 84 for separating eggs)
1–2 tablespoons cold water

FILLING
about 6–8 eating apples
12 toffee sweets

EQUIPMENT
table knife ◆ mixing bowl ◆ clingfilm
greaseproof paper ◆ 2 x 12-hole fairy cake tins
rolling pin ◆ round cutter about 8 cm across
chopping board ◆ oven gloves

SKILLS
◆ CUTTING
◆ RUBBING BUTTER INTO FLOUR
◆ LINING TART TINS WITH PASTRY
◆ SHARING FILLINGS
◆ BASHING WITH ROLLING PIN
◆ USING OVEN

STAGE
3

scones & jam

Once you know how to make scones, you will always have something for tea or for your packed lunches. Why not treat Mum and Dad and make them a batch at the weekend? Lola's friend Annabelle tested this recipe for me and made them once after breakfast and before school for her and her brother's packed lunches! Well done Annabelle!

To make 8–10 scones you need:

INGREDIENTS
225 g self-raising flour
1 teaspoon baking powder
40 g unsalted butter – chilled
1 tablespoon golden caster sugar
140–150 ml milk plus a little extra
strawberry jam, to serve

EQUIPMENT
scissors • greaseproof paper
baking tray • mixing bowl
table knife • round fluted
cutter about 6 cm across
pastry brush • oven gloves

1 Turn the oven on to 220°C (425°F) Gas 7. Cut a piece of greaseproof paper big enough to cover the baking tray. Put the flour and baking powder into a mixing bowl. Use a table knife to cut the butter into small pieces and put into the mixing bowl with the flour. Rub the butter into the flour with your fingers until it looks like fine breadcrumbs. This can take a few minutes.

2 Add the sugar and milk. Use a table knife to stir and start to mix everything together.

3 Now use your hands to bring the mixture together to make a ball of dough.

4 Sprinkle a little flour on the work surface, then tip the dough out of the bowl. Pat it gently to flatten until it is about 1.5 cm thick. Dip the cutter in flour, then cut out scones from the dough. Put the scones onto the baking tray, spaced a little apart. Gather all the spare bits of dough together, roll together to make a ball and flatten out again. Cut out the rest of the scones – you should be able to make 8, 9 or 10 scones depending on the size of your cutter.

5 Dip a pastry brush into a little milk and brush over the scones. Using oven gloves, put the scones in the oven and bake for 10 minutes until risen and golden.

Leave to cool slightly before cutting in half and serving with strawberry jam and clotted cream, if you like it.

Other good things to add to scones: For fruit scones add 50 g dried fruit, such as raisins, currants or sultanas, or chopped dried apricots or apple. Stir in when you add the sugar. Try adding a pinch of mixed spice or cinnamon. For cheesy scones, leave out the sugar and stir in 50 g grated Cheddar cheese and chopped fresh herbs.

SKILLS
- RUBBING BUTTER INTO FLOUR
- CUTTING USING CUTTERS
- BRUSHING (MILK) USING PASTRY BRUSH

STAGE
3

roasted soft fruit

When you bake fruit in the oven, the key is to not overcook it otherwise it will get too soft. The times will vary depending on the size of the fruit, but 15 minutes is good for large soft fruits like nectarines or peaches. If you choose smaller fruit like plums, cook them for just 10 minutes. Roasted fruits are great served with natural yoghurt. For a treat, add half a teaspoon of crème fraîche or double cream to each fruit half before baking so that you have a sauce at the end of the cooking time.

For 4 people you need:

INGREDIENTS
4 peaches or nectarines, or 8 plums or apricots
3 tablespoons light brown soft sugar
capful almond or vanilla extract
30 g unsalted butter

EQUIPMENT
chopping board • small paring knife • spoon
ovenproof dish • oven gloves

1 Turn the oven on to 190°C (375°F) Gas 5. Use the bridge-cutting technique to cut the fruit in half: on a chopping board, make a 'bridge' with a thumb and finger of one hand and hold the fruit. Hold a small paring knife in your other hand and put the blade under the bridge, then cut downwards firmly. You will need to move the fruit around as you cut to avoid cutting through the stone. This will take a bit of time, patience and practice.

2 Use a teaspoon to scoop the stones out of the middle of the fruit. You might need to dig the spoon under the stone to take it out.

3 Rest the fruit in an ovenproof dish with the cut side facing upwards. Spoon the sugar evenly over each fruit half, add the almond extract and dot with little pieces of the butter. Using oven gloves, put the dish in the oven and bake for 15–20 minutes. I think these peaches look so beautiful, don't you?

SKILLS
- ◆ CUTTING
- ◆ CORING FRUIT
- ◆ USING OVEN

STAGE
3

magic citrus puddings

These puddings are light and fluffy on top, with a pool of lemon sauce at the bottom. They are delicate because of the egg white, and that's why they need to be cooked in a roasting dish with water around them to help them cook slowly.

For 4–5 people you need:

INGREDIENTS
1 unwaxed lemon and 1 unwaxed lime (or just 2 lemons or limes, if you like)
100 g golden caster sugar
50 g unsalted butter – soft
2 free-range eggs
75 g self-raising flour
250 ml milk

EQUIPMENT
small grater • mixing bowl • wooden spoon • saucer • 2 bowls • balloon whisk small paring knife • electric whisk metal spoon • 4–5 small pudding basins deep baking tray • jug • oven gloves

1 Turn the oven on to 180°C (350°F) Gas 4. Using a small grater, grate the lemon and lime to make zest (see page 60 for how to do this) and put into a mixing bowl. Add the sugar and butter and mix well with a wooden spoon until it becomes fluffy and paler in colour. Crack an egg onto a saucer (see page 60 for how to do this), rest a small bowl over the yolk and tip the white into a clean bowl*. Add the egg yolk to the butter mixture in the mixing bowl and then repeat with the other egg.

2 Add the flour to the mixing bowl and, using a balloon whisk, mix together. Use the bridge-cutting technique to halve the zested lemon with a small paring knife. Squeeze the juice into the mixing bowl, add the milk and whisk.

3 Using a clean balloon whisk or an electric whisk (with help from an adult), whisk the eggs whites in their bowl until they are thick, white and make slight peaks.

5

4 Using a metal spoon, 'fold' the egg whites into the mixture in the mixing bowl. 'Folding' means to carefully cut the mixture and mix without beating all the air out of the egg whites. Fold until the whites are just mixed in.

5 Rub a little butter inside 4–5 small pudding basins and put them in a deep baking tray. Spoon the pudding mixture into the basins and then pour water from a jug into the tray to come halfway up the sides of the basins. Ask an adult to help you put the tray in the oven using oven gloves. Bake for 35 minutes, or until the puddings are light golden and cooked with a small pool of sauce in the bottom.

*Did you know that the bowl for egg whites needs to be really clean, otherwise you might not end up with fluffy egg whites?

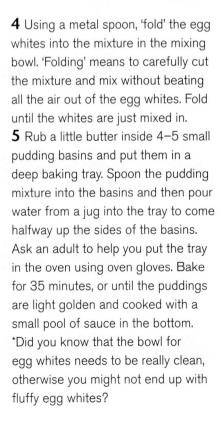

STAGE
3

blackberry pudding

This is as easy as 1, 2, 3. Weigh the ingredients, mix them together and then bake. I have chosen to use ground almonds and single cream in this recipe for a really special pudding. However, if you don't have ground almonds you could use self-raising flour and instead of cream you can use milk. It will not have the same flavour or texture, but it's still a nice pudding. You could also try to make this pudding with other fruits that are in season e.g. soft fruits like raspberries, sliced fresh peaches, plum halves or apricot halves, or mixed fruit like raspberries mixed with redcurrants and blackcurrants.

For 4 people you need:

INGREDIENTS
40 g unsalted butter
3 free-range eggs
80 g golden caster sugar
capful vanilla extract
150 ml single cream
100 g ground almonds
2 punnets blackberries
(about 350 g)
a little icing sugar for the top

EQUIPMENT
greaseproof paper • medium ovenproof dish • small saucepan • table knife big jug • fork • oven gloves

1 Turn the oven on to 180°C (350°F) Gas 4. Using a scrap of greaseproof paper, rub a little butter inside the ovenproof dish. Put the butter in a small saucepan over low heat on the hob and heat gently until it has melted. Crack the eggs into a big jug (see page 60 for how to do this) and weigh all the other ingredients.

2 Add the melted butter, sugar, vanilla extract, cream and ground almonds to the eggs in the jug and mix together with a fork. Pour this mixture into your ovenproof dish.

3 Dot the blackberries all over the mixture. Using oven gloves, put the dish into the oven and bake for 30–35 minutes or until the pudding is cooked all the way through. It tastes great with custard, ice cream or yoghurt, or on its own!

SKILLS
◆ MELTING BUTTER
◆ MIXING
◆ WEIGHING
◆ USING OVEN

STAGE
3

Ella's raspberry & white chocolate cake

Ella is the queen of Victoria sponge cakes in our house and this cake is based on a classic Victoria sponge mix. It was her idea to add fresh raspberries to the cake mix and to make some lovely big white chocolate buttons for the top. I hope you enjoy making it as much she did!

To make 1 big cake you need:

CAKE BASE
100 g white chocolate
225 g unsalted butter – soft
225 g golden caster sugar
capful vanilla extract
4 eggs – at room temperature
225 g self-raising flour
400 g ripe raspberries (or fruits of the forest) plus extra to decorate
1 teaspoon baking powder
4 tablespoons raspberry jam

BUTTERCREAM
100 g unsalted butter – soft
150 g icing sugar
3 ripe raspberries

ICING
3 ripe raspberries
250 g royal icing sugar
a little water

EQUIPMENT
2 plates • greaseproof paper • small saucepan • small heatproof bowl • oven gloves • spoon • 2 x 20-cm sandwich tins pencil • scissors • 3 mixing bowls wooden spoon • table knife • large metal spoon • fork

1

2

3

4

1 Cover a big plate with greaseproof paper. Half fill a small saucepan with water and sit a small heatroof bowl in the pan over the water (without the bowl touching the water). Break the chocolate into the small bowl. Put the pan over low heat on the hob. When the water starts to heat up, the chocolate will melt. Don't touch the chocolate – leave it until it has melted. Turn the hob off and carefully, using oven gloves, take the bowl off the pan and stir the chocolate. Spoon circles of the chocolate onto the greaseproof paper and leave somewhere cold to set.

5

6

7

2 Turn the oven on to 180°C (350°F) Gas 4. Using a scrap of greaseproof paper, rub a little butter inside the sandwich tins. Rest one tin on some greaseproof paper and draw around the tin with a pencil. Cut 2 circles out and put in the bottom of the tins.

3 Put the soft butter, sugar and vanilla extract in a mixing bowl and mix well with a wooden spoon until it becomes fluffy and paler in colour. Crack the eggs and add to the mixture a little a time, mixing all the time. Add just a little flour, too.

4 Add the raspberries and gently mix together. Don't worry if the mixture looks slightly lumpy or curdled – this is normal.

5 Add the flour and, using a large metal spoon, 'fold' it into the mixture. 'Folding' means to carefully cut the mixture and mix without beating all the air out of it.

6 Spoon the mixture equally into the tins. Using oven gloves, put the tins in the oven and bake for 20 minutes, or until the cakes are well risen and cooked through.

7 Using the oven gloves, take the cakes out of the oven. Leave to cool, then turn them out of the tins and peel the paper off. To make the buttercream, put the butter, sugar and raspberries in a bowl and mix until really smooth. Put one of the cakes onto a plate and spread the jam over it. Spread the buttercream over the jam and put the other cake on top. To make the icing, mash the raspberries in a bowl with a fork, add the royal icing sugar and a little water and mix together. Spoon onto the cake and decorate with more raspberries and the white chocolate buttons.

SKILLS
WEIGHING ◆ MEASURING
CREAMING BUTTER & SUGAR
CRACKING EGGS ◆ FOLDING
FLOUR ◆ SPREADING
MELTING CHOCOLATE

STAGE
3

pick 'n' mix hot choc

For a really special hot chocolate, you can just melt chocolate into milk like Ella is doing here and then add flavour from orange zest or a spice. Otherwise, you can use drinking chocolate powder. This is a great recipe for making when you have friends round. You can create your own 'drinks bar' with little bowls of spices or orange zest for flavour, and sweets and chocolates for the top. Your friends are likely to have great fun choosing what to add to their hot chocolates. Enjoy!

To make 1 hot chocolate you need:

HOT CHOCOLATE

milk

a few squares milk chocolate or 2 teaspoons drinking chocolate powder

FLAVOURING

freshly grated ginger, ground cinnamon, grated orange zest

TOPPING

squirty cream in a can (or whipped double cream)

a selection of sweets e.g. white chocolate buttons, milk chocolate buttons, mini-marshmallows, chocolate flakes, sprinkles

EQUIPMENT

cup • small saucepan
wooden spoon • spoon

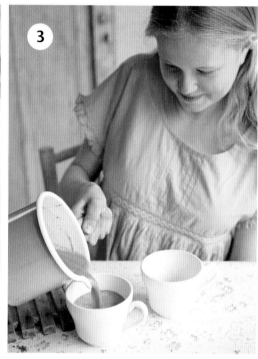

1 Measure the milk in the cup you will be using – pour the milk into your cup and then pour this milk into a small saucepan. Only three-quarters fill your cup, as you will need room for the toppings!

2 Add the chocolate to the pan and heat until it melts and the milk just starts to bubble – don't leave it too long otherwise the milk will rise up inside the pan and spill over the top! Take the pan off the heat. Stir with a wooden spoon until the chocolate has melted.

3 Pour the hot chocolate into your cup.

4 Now decide which flavour you would like to add to your hot chocolate – freshly grated ginger, ground cinnamon and grated orange zest are all good – and stir it in. Top the hot chocolate with squirty cream and chocolates and sprinkles. My children like to add a flake too!

SKILLS

MEASURING • POURING • GRATING

index

acknowledgements

Thank you so much Vicki, Alison and Leslie for making this book possible; I loved writing it! Vicki, I am particularly delighted that your lovely Lara is in some of the photos.

Ella, Lola and Finley, thank you for your ideas and for being so helpful with the recipe testing and photoshoots; I couldn't have written this book without you. I love eating the food that you cook and it is great to watch you having fun in the kitchen. David, you are still the best recipe tester and surfer (in the crescent). Dad, Liz and Mavis, thanks for your support as always and Jimmy for your helpful emails.

Well done Susan and thank you for the wonderful photographs – they are beautiful! It was a lovely, albeit fairly exhausting way to begin the year. Iona, thank you again for all your help and your great design. Brenda and Esther, we couldn't have done the shoots without your help – thank you both! Céline, thank you once again – I really admire your attention to detail. Jo, you may have been in the background but your help was invaluable, thank you.

Thanks too to Jess and the gorgeous children in the book. It is very special having friends in the photos – Ella, Lola & Finley; Ishbel & Sholto; Aisha; Amy; Bea & Frankie, Betty, Bob & Hector; Emily; Hannah & Maya; Lara; Mickey; Molly & Oscar; Pia & Isabelle; Sadie; Sam; Thomas. On that note, a big thank you to Mr Elliot, our fantastic Head teacher at Southover Primary School, for your support. Now all we need to do is get cooking classes going at school…

Thank you to Anita McCormac, OBE, Director of the Focus on Food Campaign, for your help and support. I think the Campaign is amazing and I truly admire all the work you are doing to help the next generation to select, prepare and cook healthy food.

A huge thank you to Penelope Leach. I was utterly thrilled when you agreed to read parts of this book; thank you for your constructive feedback and your quote. I feel honoured.

Marguerite, it was the highlight of my career to have a chat with you at your home. I think you are an inspiration and your quote in my book is like the icing on the cake.

A big thank you to the following shops for helping with the lovely props in this book

Churchill Antique Centre +44(0)1273 474842

Lewes Antique Centre +44(0)1273 476148

Cath Kidston +44(0)8450 262 440
www.cathkidston.co.uk

Cabbages & Roses + 44(0)20 7352 7333
www.cabbagesandroses.com

Steamer Trading Cookshop +44(0)1273 403000
www.steamer.co.uk

Wickle +44(0)1273 487969
www.wickle.co.uk

Pots and pans +44(0)1877 332 701
www.pots-and-pans.co.uk

RE +44(0)1434 634567
www.re-foundobjects.com

Au Maison www.aumaison.dk